D0961401

Life After Darkness

ALSO BY MICHELLE KNIGHT

Finding Me: A Decade of Darkness, a Life Reclaimed

Life After Darkness

*Finding Healing and
Happiness After the
Cleveland Kidnappings*

Michelle Knight

NOW KNOWN AS

Lily Rose Lee

NEW YORK   BOSTON

Hachette Books
Hachette Book Group
1290 Avenue of the Americas, New York, NY 10104
hachettebooks.com
twitter.com/hachettebooks

First Edition: May 2018

Hachette Books is a division of Hachette Book Group, Inc. The Hachette Books name and logo are trademarks of Hachette Book Group, Inc.

The publisher is not responsible for websites (or their content) that are not owned by the publisher.

The Hachette Speakers Bureau provides a wide range of authors for speaking events. To find out more, go to www.hachettespeakersbureau.com or call (866) 376-6591.

Editorial production by Christine Marra, Marrathon Production Services. www.marrathoneditorial.org

Book design by Jane Raese
Set in 12-point ITC New Baskerville

Library of Congress Control Number: 2018930201

ISBN 978-1-60286-564-8 (hardcover); ISBN 978-1-60286-575-4 (ebook)

Printed in the United States of America

LSC-C

10 9 8 7 6 5 4 3 2 1

For Miguel, for all that he is.

And for Joey, wherever he is.

Contents

Preface

I'm proud of my heart and who I have become . . .

My name is Lillian Rose Lee—Lily for short.

That is not the name I was born with. It is the name I was *reborn* with.

Lillian Rose Lee is the name I gave myself when I decided that I alone am in control of my life, when I determined that no one else would ever have power over me again.

Lillian Rose Lee is who I feel I am.

You may know me by another name: Michelle Knight. That was my name when, at the age of twenty-one, I was kidnapped and held captive by a brutal and probably insane man named Ariel Castro. For eleven years, nearly four thousand days, I was chained, sexually abused, and beaten—day after day, months on end, year after year. I lived in filth in a house without windows, was fed spoiled or rotten food when

I was fed at all, and was prevented from learning anything of the outside world. I was impregnated five times, and five times Castro beat or starved me into miscarriage. He kidnapped two other women as well; I was chained to one of them for much of the time during those eleven years.

I was rescued on May 6, 2013. I walked out of that dark, filthy house of horrors into the light and fell to my knees. I fell partly because after eleven years of being immobilized I was physically weak and partly because I was almost blinded by the sunshine. Mostly, I went down on my knees so I could thank God I had survived. I was alive, and I was free.

That freedom felt like an explosion. Can you imagine what it was like, after eleven years, to know I was no longer a prisoner bound with chains who had to ask permission to move and who was afraid to say what I was thinking or risk getting beaten? Now, all on my own, I could choose to sit or stand, to stay or go, to talk or stay quiet. I could decide what I did, where I went, how I lived. I could even create a life for myself, maybe a normal life, maybe a life in which I could find happiness.

But if you had asked me then how to do that—how to come back from horror and create a normal life—I would not have been able to answer you. I was free, yes. Free in the sense that I knew that no one was going to rape me that day. Or the next. Or the day after that. Or ever again. After what I had lived through, knowing that the terror was over was like having the weight of the earth lifted off my shoulders. But when it came to building a life after all the darkness I had been through, I was basically starting from scratch. I had no idea how or where to begin. Nothing in those eleven years and, frankly, little in my life before those years had prepared me to seek or create a normal, happy life—nothing except a survivor's grit.

FIVE YEARS have passed since my rescue, and I know many of you have wondered how I've gotten along and what has become of me. I regularly get questions from readers of *Finding Me*, from people who know me through social media, and from many people who simply remember the story of the "three girls" from the house of horrors in Cleveland. They want to know how I'm doing and what I'm doing. They ask about my son, Joey, about my relationship with the other two women held captive with me, Gina DeJesus and Amanda Berry, and about whether I have reconciled with my family. Fair questions, but the answers are complicated.

They wonder also if I have confronted problems in moving forward, if I have found a way to heal my wounds, and if I have been able to form any relationships with men. I can tell you that in one sense, the answer to all three of these questions is yes, but the stories behind those yeses can get pretty complex.

I realized it would take another book to answer these and other questions. That's the book you have in your hands right now.

THE WORLD I entered when I got out of captivity had moved on without me for more than a decade. It was a strange new place. And I didn't have a lot going for me to help me navigate this new world.

For one thing, I was pretty sick. Gina and Amanda were released from the hospital that we were all taken to a day after we were admitted. I was in and out of hospitals for weeks.

Also, when Gina and Amanda were released from the hospital, they went *home*. Their families greeted them with banners and celebrations, with hugs and tears. I had no home to return to, no family to take me in. Most people think of family as the people nearest and dearest to you, the people who nurture and protect you. They think of home as a place of warmth and safety. I never had such a family or such a home. Not even close. The household I grew up in was never a safe haven; it's where I was first harmed. My "family" was a collection of people who came and went without caring or kindness. But I do recall one grownup, a classmate's mother, who showed me kindness and warmth. Her name is Rose. I chose it as part of my own name for the new life I am creating.

The only family I was desperately longing to see was my son, Joey. He was thirteen the day I walked out of Castro's house. He had been taken from me even before Castro took me from him. In fact, I was on my way to a meeting about regaining custody of my son when I was abducted. But I always assumed that freedom meant I would be able to find him again, that somehow we could be reunited, and that I would truly be home. I didn't know then and wouldn't know for several weeks that Joey had been adopted by a loving family years before. I was not allowed to know where he was or anything about his new family.

So I was very much on my own as I lay in my hospital bed in Cleveland's MetroHealth Medical Center after being rescued. On my own and with few resources. Yes, our rescue ignited an immediate and overwhelming public response. My hospital room was soon flooded with gifts and flowers from complete strangers, and donations to what was called the Cleveland Courage Fund were enough to create trusts that still provide financial support. I will always be grateful to all the people whose heartfelt help was so important to all of us getting back on our feet. It was the first time I ever felt that people who didn't know me could care about me.

That realization warmed and strengthened me, but there were other realities that weren't so pretty. I was thirty-two years old and had lost all of my twenties—probably the most robust years of any human being's life—to Castro and captivity. My body was broken. My heart was torn apart. My mind had been challenged to its limits. I was frail and exhausted. And I was alone. I had a long way to go and a lot of healing to do if I was to build a new life after darkness.

Healing doesn't happen overnight. It is a process that takes time and moves in stages. I had to nurse the wounds, some of them very deep, that went all the way back to my childhood. I had to treat the injuries from years of suffering, even if I couldn't make the scars disappear. I had to soothe the pain and, in some cases, such as the pain from the loss of my son, learn to live with it.

I made my share of mistakes along the way. There were people I trusted I should not have trusted, things I did that I wish I could undo, moves I made I would like to roll back. I can't.

But survivor's grit teaches you how to turn mistakes into strengths. I picked myself up and kept going. And I had help along the way: legal help, financial help, and a whole team of folks helping me put together *Finding Me*, then helping me cope with the nuts and bolts of book tours and public appearances and the celebrity that came with it.

And then there were the well-wishers. The people who came up to me after a talk about abuse or domestic violence or missing children and thanked me. The people who stopped me in the street and gave me a hug, the people who told me I "inspired" them, the people who, to this day, shake my hand and tell me they hope I will be reunited with my son. Every good wish, every warm thought makes a difference.

SOMETHING ELSE has made a difference both in strengthening me and in helping my healing process: the growing power of abuse victims to speak up and speak out. Women especially—and never more so than in the months leading up to the publication of this book—have found their voice when it comes to every form of harassment, assault, and the misuse of power. Suddenly it seems that everywhere you look—in entertainment, business, government, politics, sports—women and girls are calling out the powerful men who demeaned them, hurt their careers, created toxic work environments, abused their trust, dishonored their bodies.

I welcome all these women and girls to the fight that I too have been waging since my rescue five years ago. I believe it is this swelling chorus of survivors' voices that has brought about what I see as the beginning of a profound change in perception and attitude around the country and the world. The cat is now out of the bag: no one can ever again say they had no idea this was happening. The more women and girls tell their stories, the more others who have suffered abuse will hear it. The more they hear it, the more they will be encouraged to speak up on their own behalf.

As you'll read in the pages that follow, until every victim of abuse is able to do that, I have made it my life's work to speak out for them. Advocacy on behalf of those who suffered or may now be suffering the kinds of physical, sexual, and mental abuse that I suffered is today the inspiration of my life. Given my own escape and the life I have made for myself after the darkness, I consider it a blessing to be able to advocate while bringing hope to survivors, and I will continue to do so as long as I am able.

BUT WHAT really has powered my healing and what graces the life I have built after darkness is love. That is why this second book, *Life After Darkness*, is, above all, a love story. Not just because it tells how I found "my sweetie," the love of my life and my soul's companion. That was something I never even dreamed possible when I was rescued. But it has happened, and it has been the great happiness of my life.

At the same time this is a love story because it is about the power of love to heal suffering and pain and to transform and empower us. I mean the love my friend's mother Rose showed me—a shining spark of light in a bleak and otherwise loveless childhood that gave me strength. The love for my son that steeled me to stay alive during eleven brutal years. The love of the true friends I eventually did find who are now such a blessing in my life—my safe circle. There is nothing better than knowing you are loved for yourself alone.

Above all, I mean the love I was able to open myself to that has magnified the love I want to give—to the son I hope to find some day, to my friends, to my husband, and to that other person deserving of love: myself. Love is what lights up my life after darkness.

Life After Darkness

CHAPTER ONE

Free!

I am grateful for every day and every night I am able to see the sunrise and the sunset . . .

WHEN YOU'VE SPENT eleven years in hell, you don't take anything for granted ever again. Not one single thing—no matter how small.

Waking up in a clean, warm bed in a safe home is heaven to me. Being able to take a shower, to comb my hair, to brush my teeth, to take my time adding the right amount of cream and sugar into my coffee so it's just the way I like it—that's paradise. I thank God for these blessings every day. I appreciate each as it is happening.

Almost every morning now I start the day by taking my cup of coffee out back behind the house—either onto the deck where I settle into my rocking chair or right into the yard—and just take in what I see, hear, and feel all around me. I want to immerse myself in the sights and sounds, to feel the freedom, to taste every small pleasure as deeply as I can.

I bring the dogs with me and watch them play catch. All four of them: the three mutts, Rascal, Cupid, and Faith, and my purebred pit bull, Peanut. They are sweet, loving animals, and they can be pretty goofy as they run around catching and dropping the ball. It is their favorite game, and watching them at play gives me joy from the top of my head to the bottom of my toes. While they race around playing, I watch the sun rise and listen to the birds flying by or the ones in the trees chirping, or to the sounds of children laughing from over the fence, or of leaves rustling in the breeze. I might catch a glimpse of a bunny or a deer walking by or feel the wind in my hair. I let these sensations soak into my skin, and

I cherish the peace of these moments. Nobody knows better than I do that in the blink of an eye, it can all disappear.

If it's warm enough, I'll sit in one of the chairs we've arranged around what I think of as the heart of our yard—a man-made pond, full of fish, with a little waterfall. At the top of the waterfall is a sculpture of a guardian angel with a little boy. This is to remind me that wherever my son Joey is, an angel is watching over him for me. Around the pond are five additional angels, each representing one of the babies I lost. These angels look over my pond and fish and, I hope, the dogs and all the other critters and living things, including us. On the rocks that circle the pond there is a sculpture that says "Welcome," and there are pots of all my favorite flowers—lilies, my namesake flowers, plus tubs of roses and carnations. You can usually spot some of the dogs' toys on the rocks as well. We have planted a ring of bushes around all of this, and beyond the bushes we have planted a ring of trees to add to the mature, solid, really tall and big trees already there.

To just sit like this, with my hands around a hot cup of coffee flavored just the way I like, probably sounds like a pretty ordinary pastime to most people. But it never stops being extraordinary to me. To me, this moment of quiet is a gift from God. I can sit out here forever just being grateful for the peace, knowing that I can write and draw whatever and whenever I want, that there's a store I can go to whenever I run out of anything I need, that I can watch each of the plants I have personally put in the ground take root and grow, each one as unique in shape and color as every human is unique.

Even in our cold Cleveland winters, when the weather forecasters warn us about the arctic air heading down from Canada and shooting off Lake Erie, making it as chilly as you can imagine, I spend mornings as close as I can to being outside in the backyard. I'll plug in an electric blanket and wrap it around me when it gets really frigid, and if it ever gets just too cold to sit out there, I scrunch up indoors in front of the window and just watch and listen. I do this because after being rescued from brutal captivity, being alive and free and knowing that I will wake up just as alive and free tomorrow is an answered prayer, and every day I treasure the knowledge and draw strength from it.

THE CAPTIVITY began in 2002. I was Michelle Knight then, a twenty-one-year-old single mother living in Cleveland, Ohio, and trying to regain custody of my son, Joey. I lost custody when I left Joey with my mother so I could go job hunting, and my mother's boyfriend lashed out at my two-year-old, fracturing his knee. Of course, the hospital called social services, social services investigated, and Joey was assigned to foster care, which meant they kept moving him from one home to another.

It was August, and there was going to be a court hearing at the end of the month when I was going to try to win Joey

back. I was on my way to Joey's latest foster home to see him
and meet with social services, and I was lost.

The address for the foster home was in a part of town I
didn't know well, it was hot, and I was going to be late, which
was the last thing I needed if I was going to get my son back.
I saw a Family Dollar store up ahead, went inside, showed
the address to a couple of the sales clerks, and asked if they
could help, but nobody knew where the place was.

"I know exactly where it is," said a male voice, and I
turned and saw Ariel Castro, the father of a girl I had gone
to school with. I said hello and reminded him of our connection, and Castro offered to drive me to the house where
Joey was living. Instead, of course, he drove me to his own
house—surrounded by a locked fence, with dark windows,
some of which looked like they were covered in dark plastic.
He needed to get something, he said, unlocking the back
door, and oh, he had some puppies I might want to see—
maybe he could give me one for my son, so why didn't I
come on inside with him, as it would only take a minute.

The date was August 23, 2002. I was a prisoner in that
house until May 6, 2013.

For eleven years, season after season, I was confined in
that filthy house of horrors. Mostly, I was chained to one
place, unable to move very far, if at all. Daily, Castro beat
and sexually abused me. In 2003 Castro kidnapped Amanda
Berry. In 2004 he kidnapped Gina DeJesus. The police
looked for Amanda and Gina. Their families looked for
them, worried about them, cried over them. My family fig-

ured I had run away or had simply left town—or maybe they didn't think anything at all, just that I wasn't around anymore. In any event, no one ever looked for me.

Of course, Amanda, Gina, and I forged a connection. We were all pawns in Castro's terrible game, sister sufferers in the little kingdom he ruled, his grotesque, insane kingdom of injury and hurt. But all of us knew that I was the one he tortured the most. I was the one who bore the brunt of his beatings: he slammed a barbell against my jaw and across the side of my head, and when I became pregnant—five times— he beat me, starved me, and one time actually hurled me down the stairs until I miscarried. So by the time I was thirty years old I had lost six babies: my Joey and the five fetuses Castro tortured out of me.

When Amanda became pregnant, Castro did not force her to miscarry. And when she went into labor, he made me act as midwife of the birth because I was the only one who knew anything at all about the process. The birth was rough, but it brought a beautiful child into our lives. She was a tiny affirmation of life in the midst of all the misery and squalor, and she was a reminder—which we desperately needed—that there really can be such a thing in the world as joy.

Many, many times during those eleven years I was afraid I was going to die. And many times I was in such despair that I was afraid I was *not* going to die. What kept me alive was my love for my son. Thinking about him, imagining him growing up, talking to him in my dreams, creating poems to him and about him in my mind and later writing the poems down on the scraps of paper Castro let me have: in the end I could put up with anything so long as I held to the hope that my son was all right, that he was being cared for somewhere by someone, and that I would one day see him again.

On May 6, 2013, all of us—me, Gina, Amanda, and Amanda's daughter, now six years old—were freed. A daring move by Amanda made our escape possible. She found a small opening in the outside storm door on the main floor of the house, big enough that she could extend her arm through it. Waving and shouting, she caught the attention of neighbors across the street. Amanda worked the bottom panel of the door loose, crawled through, and then pulled her daughter through. Someone called 911, and a police car drove up to Castro's house, where Gina and I were still barricaded in our upstairs bedroom.

We had no idea that it was cops who were making the noise we heard downstairs. We did not know that Amanda was no longer in the house. We certainly did not know she had called for help. The neighborhood was a tough one. Drug crime was rampant. So when we heard sudden and unexplained movements downstairs, and someone yelled, "We're the police," we had no reason to believe it was true.

I was so terrified that I fled into the next room and hid behind a cabinet. "Anybody in here?" a man's voice asked from behind the door. Then the door opened. The man and a woman entered. Blue uniforms, guns on their hips, silver badges.

I don't know—I don't think I will ever remember—if I let out a scream or made any sound at all, but my body propelled itself forward like a rocket onto the body of that poor woman police officer. I threw my arms around her neck. "Please don't let go of me," I begged, and I clung to her for dear life.

Dear life was exactly what it was. Eleven grim and lonely years, filled with misery and pain, both mental and physical, and empty of anything that makes life worth living, had just ended. In a split second, life seemed possible again.

When I finally let go of the police officer and made my way downstairs, I saw another police officer holding open the front door that Amanda had managed to break a hole in. I walked through the door and down the porch steps. I had never been on the porch; I had seen it eleven years before, when Ariel Castro pulled up to the house "to get something" before driving me to see my son. I never got to the appointment, had not seen my son in eleven years, and had lived through hell all that time. No wonder I fell to my knees as soon as my feet cleared the porch. I thanked God for my delivery, then climbed through the open back doors of the waiting ambulance.

Amanda and her daughter were there. "Are you okay, Juju?" Amanda's daughter asked me now, using her pet name for me. It was such a simple, innocent question. I nodded *yes, I'm okay,* and then I began to sob.

Amanda grabbed my hand. "We're free!" she cried. "We're free now! We're going home!" Then Gina climbed into the ambulance, and the three of us hugged and wept.

One of the ambulance guys took my temperature, then wrapped me in a blanket and asked my name. "Michelle Knight," I said.

"Michelle, I'm going to set you up with some oxygen." He motioned for me to lie down, then put a mask over my face. But my face was so bruised and swollen—my entire jaw was black and blue all over—that the mask actually hurt. I breathed in and instantly felt woozy. Then I felt an injection in my arm—it was epinephrine—and I just let go. Whatever terror I was still holding onto from the morning flowed out of me as fast as the epi was shooting into me. For the first time in more than eleven years someone kind and caring was attending to me. The nightmare was over.

CHAPTER TWO

An Impatient Patient

*You never know how strong you are until being
strong is the only choice you have—and giving up
is not an option . . .*

OUR RESCUE MADE news all over the country and all around the world. The human fascination with horror is as strong as the human desire for a so-called happy ending to the horror, and I suppose that is what powered all that news coverage.

We were certainly the biggest story in all of the Midwest that night, just as we were the biggest, most blaring headline in all the papers the next morning. I didn't see much of the news coverage at the time—I was too out of it. But our rescue continued to make news for a long, long time as the media "followed up" on the story six months later and again on the first-year anniversary of our rescue, and again and again over the years. We're not the only survivors of abduction and imprisonment to have their lives recorded in this way; you often see reports on what has become of people who suffered as we did, reports about how we're doing and how well we are getting on with our lives—or not. And certainly whenever a similar abduction is reported, our story and similar past stories are brought up again as background.

But if you watch on YouTube the local TV broadcasts of that night—May 6, 2013—you can see the shock and excitement of the day all over again. It feels like all of Cleveland was tuned in to the television newscasts, and clearly the local newscasters—every one of them—were beside themselves. All were shocked by the horror of what had happened to the three of us. All reported triumphantly on the rescue and endlessly replayed Amanda's phone call to the 911 operator, who seemed confused and couldn't quite get what Amanda was saying. But the saving grace of the story, the heartwarming "ending" everyone wanted to see, was in the reports by newscasters stationed at the emergency room entrance of the big public hospital, MetroHealth Center, where the ambulance had taken us. You could hear the happy relief and the thrill in the news reporters' voices as they told how "the three girls" had been reunited with the families who had never given up hope, families who had held annual candlelight vigils for their missing daughters, sisters, nieces, cousins—families who at that moment were lavishing "loving attention" on the beloved children who had been rescued and returned to them.

Not my family. After all, they had never lavished loving attention on me when I lived at home as a child; there was pretty much no reason for them to start now. As far as I could tell, my family had barely noticed I was gone, and there were no family members in the hospital waiting room, at least not on that night.

Not that I would have noticed if they had been there. Like I said, I was pretty out of it. I don't know to this day what was flowing into me intravenously—"powerful antibiotics" was all I heard. I would later learn that I weighed in at just about eighty-four pounds when I arrived at the hospital. Eleven years of confinement, of being restrained by chains, of torture and beatings and squalor had done their work. I was very, very weak and very, very sick.

Anybody who has ever been in a hospital knows there's always a light on somewhere, so it's never totally dark at night, and there's always some sort of noise, so it's never totally quiet. You're left with a kind of low-level buzz of activity. The buzz can sometimes help lull you to sleep in a way, sort of releasing you from having to look or listen or think too hard. All your senses more or less relax, whether you want them to or not. That first night out of Castro's house, that hospital buzz was going strong. Drugs of one sort or another were pouring into me. I wasn't entirely sure what the doctors were thinking or doing, and I had absolutely no idea what was next for me. I barely knew what time it was or whether it was day or night. But still, through the haze of all the lights, through the clacking sound of footsteps up and down the corridor outside my hospital room, through the beeping sounds of monitors, through the dim recognition of a nurse holding my wrist and taking my pulse, I was totally aware of one thing above all: I was free. I knew the way I know my own flesh that I had been rescued. I sensed that Castro would now pay for his unspeakable crimes, and if I could have shouted, I would have—to tell the world that I had survived the darkness.

The next day I learned that Amanda and Gina had been released from the hospital and had gone home. I was on my own.

It felt right. I had survived the darkness, and out there in the light, a life was waiting for me. It was up to me to get better and strong so I could get out there and grab it.

Yet at the moment, as I would not learn until much later, I was closer to death than I realized. My fever wasn't coming down, my digestive tract was a disaster, and I was in so much pain that I would wake up certain I was being stabbed. The doctors actually thought I might die. I disagreed. *I am not going to die today,* I told myself, *and I am not going to die tomorrow.* I figured there had to be a reason I had been freed from that house, and I needed to live so I could fulfill whatever purpose had kept me alive.

Mostly I believed the purpose was my son, Joey. He was the reason I had stayed alive, and he was the reason I needed to get better. When I finally felt like I would make sense if I talked, the first thing that came out of my mouth was to ask the nurse if there was somebody that could find my son. "I need to let my son know I'm alive," I said. The nurse called in a police officer who was outside my room, and the officer asked me Joey's name and date of birth and some other questions and said he would turn the matter over to a detective. Then I fell back half-asleep.

The police were not the only people in and out of my hospital room. The FBI was there too. Ariel Castro had been arrested, and FBI investigators were starting to build the case against him. The problem for me was that the lesson of my childhood had been that "telling" was worse than keeping silent. *Children should be seen and not heard* was what I was told over and over again in our household. I had heard it so many times that it was almost carved into my brain. I hadn't *just* heard the words; they had been demonstrated to me: every time I had reached out for help as a child by trying to talk to someone in authority, I had been punished one way or another. Hours after being freed from Castro's hell, I was both afraid to speak and afraid not to.

And I was being asked to speak a lot. Over those first days in the hospital a steady stream of cops and various officials and doctors were asking me question after question—often the same question in different ways. After a while I just wanted to scream. I was exhausted and needed peace and quiet if I was going to be able to hear anything. I just wanted to be left alone. At the same time I was terrified that Castro would somehow go free. I desperately wanted to find out where Joey was. And, of course, I wanted to get well. So I answered as best I could.

The doctors were doing a lot more than asking questions. They were running tests, but the fact that I couldn't bear for any male to touch me or even to come near me didn't make the job easy for them. So a whole bunch of women doctors and nurses were the ones to stick needles into my arms, push and poke various parts of my body, order me to sit or bend or look up or look down. There were X-rays, blood tests, CT scans, eye tests, hearing tests, and more. I no longer remember the number or names of the diagnostic tests I was given, just that they seemed to go on forever. One blessed benefit was that on day two in the hospital I took a long, hot shower. My first real shower in a decade. I remember standing under the water in that clean, steamy bathroom, knowing I could stand there as long as I wanted—it felt just wonderful. But the scrubbing also revealed a lot more bruises all over my body.

The tests revealed a lot too. They showed there was serious injury to my jaw. It's the reason a lot of people thought I talked funny: when someone punches you repeatedly in the face or socks your jaw with a barbell, it can really mess up your ability to form some words. Also, being chained at the ankle, wrist, stomach, or around the neck almost daily for eleven years and being thrown down stairs and across rooms resulted in serious numbness and sciatic nerve damage from my back through my hips to my knees and ankles. My toes were broken numerous times and never really healed. One hand was also damaged; the doctors thought the thumb had been fractured and had mended wrong. To this day it's hard to feel with that hand, and I need to be careful picking up a phone or holding my coffee cup so I don't drop it.

My eyes were never great, but being kept mostly in the dark for eleven years made them worse. There is nerve damage under the lenses of the eyes, so I am extremely sensitive to light. My hearing in one ear was nearly shot; it's my left ear, which was the side of my head that received so many blows, including with the barbell. I still sometimes have to lean to one side to hear better, and people think I'm ignoring them or not listening. But it's just the opposite: I'm leaning that way because I am trying hard to listen. The worst problem was my digestion, and all during those first four days in the hospital, despite a whole bunch of different doctors taking different tests, they still couldn't figure out precisely what was wrong.

There was also a parade of people coming into the room bringing things—bouquets of flowers, balloons, and various gifts. I was amazed by all of it, and I was moved beyond belief by the thought of so many people wanting to reach out with such kindness, so many people wanting to tell me they noticed me and cared about me. For someone who had never been noticed or cared for, those first days of freedom were overwhelming.

I also learned that people were donating money to the three of us and that a fund was being established to manage all the donations. "Get a lawyer," someone told me, and some of the FBI and hospital personnel quickly helped me choose one. "Help me find my son," I begged a female FBI agent, and she said she would try.

My mind could barely make sense of the fact that the horror was over. Managing all the other things that were suddenly going on—my medical situation, the outpouring of care from people whose names I didn't know, the presence of cops and FBI agents and officials and lawyers—was all a bit too much. I couldn't get my head around it. For eleven years I had measured my days by the abuse being done to me. The routine was brutal, but it was simple, and I expected it. Not knowing what to expect was a shock to my system.

The second day in the hospital, after Amanda and Gina were released, one of my brothers came to see me. I hadn't seen him since he was a little boy, and now he was a grown man. I was glad to see him; we hugged and cried at being together again. He told me he hadn't even known I was missing. My mother had told him I had left. My aunt had told him I had probably run away. He did not know where Joey was, and he had no idea that I would never have willingly left my son. Never. He just knew that no one had ever bothered to look for either of us; their lives just kept going. Kind of like: easy come, easy go. Your sister or daughter and her little boy stop showing up one day—no big deal, move on.

My brother shared with me various pieces of "news" about this or that member of our family, and I soon began to feel anxious, which was the last thing I needed given how ill I already was. Just about everything he told me brought up really bad memories and fired up all the old questions about my family life. It was all just too much too soon. I was sick enough, I decided, without being reminded of a distressing childhood. "I'm sorry," I told my brother. "You have to leave. It's not your fault, but I need time. I need to think, and I need to take care of myself." The moment I said that, I realized how true it was: I really did need to take care of myself.

I felt bad about sending him away. I did not know that he too was going through a very tough time just then. He had no place to go. He had let himself follow a dark road to try to get away from the pain he had also suffered in our childhood. To this day I do not know where my brother is or how he is coping.

I had barely settled down from my brother's visit when my aunt showed up. I didn't want to see her. She was another reminder of the awful childhood I wanted to forget. But I finally agreed to let her in, and she told me that my mother had moved to Florida, that the cousin I had lived with when I was kidnapped was now in New York, that other family members had dispersed, that the place we all had lived in when I was a kid had been torn down and replaced by condos. Good riddance, I thought. That was not a house worth preserving. And now everyone in it had moved on as if I had never existed. Fine. There could be no room for them in my new life. "No more," I told my aunt. "No more disrespect, no more hurting one another. When you're ready to deal with me on those terms, call me."

These "family visits" had been totally nerve wracking, not exactly the kind of medicine or therapy you'd prescribe for a sick person who has just escaped a nightmare. I told one of the nurses—my favorite, Marie, who was amazingly kind and sweet—that I had had it with my family. "Hon," I said to her, "I don't want to deal with this. I need time to cope. Please don't let any more of them in here." She promised, and she was as good as her word.

Between the officials and the family and the doctors, I was glad for some time alone. I sensed I needed it. My head was cloudy with terrible memories and awful new realities— no word of Joey, no family, no real home, my body broken, no one to trust.

But later that day or the next I felt a presence in my hospital room. "Is it okay if I sit with you?" a gentle female voice asked. I opened my eyes to see a woman a decade or two older than me; she told me she was there as an advocate for abducted children. Her name was Miss Pointer, and, as I found out later, she had come to this advocacy work for the terrible reason that her own daughter had been abducted and murdered; in fact, just a few days before, on the very day I was freed, she had learned that her daughter's murderer had at long last been apprehended and was in custody. But that day she gave no hint of this as she came in and sat beside me. She simply said she didn't see any family surrounding me and wanted to keep me company, if I would like, and then she just began to sing—in a rich and beautiful voice.

"Do you know the song 'Lift Every Voice and Sing'?" I asked her. I knew that it was considered a kind of African American anthem, and Miss Pointer is African American, so I thought she might know it. And she did. She began to sing, and I sang with her. I'm not sure our rejoicing rose "high as the listening skies," as the song says, but I do know that for the length of the song, my hospital room rang "with the harmonies of liberty." Miss Pointer entered my life that day with great grace, and she has never left. I am, she says, her "sister from another mister"—we are soul mates.

In all, I spent four days in MetroHealth, and it was hard work. I don't just mean the medical interventions; after all, they're what started to bring me back from the brink to where I could begin to regain my health and my strength. I mean the psychological toil of trying to adjust—basically overnight—from captivity to freedom, from being tortured to being cared for, from no life to life. I mean the very heavy emotional burden of trying to deal with all of that *and* trying to find out about my son *and* trying to cope with my family maneuvering their way back into my life.

One of the hardest things I had to do came toward the end of the four days when I was summoned to my official FBI interview. The interview took place in a special room in the hospital; I was still hooked up to IVs, so I walked slowly down the hospital corridors with my IV pole rolling next to me. Two female FBI agents were asking the questions, and I believe other agents were behind what I guessed was a two-way observation mirror in another room. The interview went on for hours. The notebooks I had kept had been retrieved from Castro's house, and the agents took me through each of the eleven years, one year at a time. They were patient but painstaking, and they asked a seemingly endless number of questions; it was a little bit like living the whole ordeal all over again. But I was aware that what they learned would help put Castro away forever, so I stuck it out. As it turned out, this was just the first interview—I would be called back to clarify many points. But that first interview was exhausting and emotionally difficult.

On my last day in the MetroHealth Center my mother came to the hospital to visit. I already knew she had traveled back to Ohio from Florida—right into the headlines, in fact, as her arrival sparked a whole new flurry of press stories. Some reporter or other dredged up a Missing Persons report that someone in my family—I still don't know who—had filed when he or she noticed I wasn't around some eleven years before. Whoever it was apparently told the cops that I had a mental condition and was frequently confused by my surroundings. This prompted a group of doctors to come into my room to give me tests that would check my intelligence and mental state. "I'm not taking your tests," I told them. "I don't have to prove anything to you or anybody else."

They backed off, but they didn't get it. They didn't know what I knew: the tests wouldn't change their minds. I knew this because I'd been there before; I'd gone through it all my life.

Not anymore. I was done with anyone else making choices for me. And I was as done as I could be with my family.

When the hospital officials told me my mother was here to visit, I refused to see her. This was the first time I had ever said no to my mother. It felt right.

After four days at MetroHealth my overall health had improved, although not much. I was a little bit stronger, and it looked like some of my bruises were beginning to mend, but there was still no clear diagnosis of what was wrong with my digestion, and that was a major worry. The doctors determined that I should be transferred to hospice care and assigned me to an assisted-living facility in Hinckley, Ohio. The place was about an hour's drive from Cleveland but kind of in the country. I distributed my flowers, balloons, and many of my gifts to the other patients, especially a few who, I had learned, had no visitors at all. When it was time to say goodbye to Marie, she gave me a present: a necklace with a cross that had a heart fixed to it. She put the necklace around my neck, and every day after that, I held the cross, praying I would stay alive, get well, and one day see my son. I still do that every day just before I go to bed—hold the gift she gave me in my hands and pray the prayer. This is what I pray:

> As I lay me down to sleep, I pray that my hope never fades and that my faith is never shaken. I pray that the Lord will take my pain and the pain of so many others and that he will shed light on our darkness and guide our hand and heart and allow us to see brighter days. If I should die before I wake, my only prayer is that God keep my son safe. Give him the life that I never had, filled with love, happiness, and serenity. That is what I always wanted for you, my little angel, and I tried everything in my power to give you that. I will always stay strong until the day that I meet you and can fill the space in my heart. My Lord, I ask you for the courage to face my demons and conquer them head-on, to learn from the mistakes I made so I can swallow my fear and live life with my pride and my faith still intact, and to share my life experience so others may know that our past doesn't define who we are.

The drive to the assisted-living facility was a revelation. My hometown was almost unrecognizable. Whole new neighborhoods had sprung up, with whole new houses and parks and playgrounds. Cleveland's downtown, with pedestrian malls, glass-covered skyscrapers, and a new look for the city buses, struck me as almost futuristic. I wept as I realized with a shock how much of life I had missed.

CHAPTER THREE

Transition: Assisted Living

I may make mistakes. I may fall on my butt
a time or two. But I know I can get back up,
dust myself off, and give myself grace. And I know
that I have positive people in my life to support
and understand me . . .

GOING INTO HOSPICE care probably seems like a strange way to get back into the real world or to build a new life after eleven years of torture and fear. And the truth is that when I think back on the six months I spent in that assisted-living residence in Hinckley, I myself am a little unsure how to judge the experience. I think some sort of intermission was probably a good idea. It would have been a real shock to the system, I think, to go directly from the hell I had been through into a world I couldn't recognize, a world nothing like the one I had left eleven years before, and try to function like everybody else. I needed some sort of transition, and the hospice, where I was partly being cared for and partly on my own, was probably as good as any transition I could find.

My new lawyer drove me to the facility. The trunk of her car was stuffed to the brim with many of the gifts and cards I had received from hundreds of well-wishers while I was in the hospital. I didn't have much in the way of a wardrobe for myself, but I had several dozen teddy bears: not much to wear, but lots to hug. When we arrived I took a long look at the "facility," a big, sort of ordinary-looking house, and thought to myself, *I guess this is home. For now.*

Where else could I go? I had no real home to return to and no family or friends to help me, and I was too sick at first to attempt much of anything. I just wasn't prepared to start finding an apartment, thinking about a job, trying to connect with people. The hospice gave me time to regain my physical health and rebuild my strength psychologically so I would be better prepared—or so I hoped—to go out on my own.

There was something else too. The place offered a sense of security I had never really known before. I had certainly never felt free from danger or from the threat of danger when I was growing up at home. When I ran away and was living on the streets I felt secure in the sense that at least no one was going to abuse me as they had at home. But on the streets you never know what is going to happen next, and that's not a very secure feeling.

At the assisted-living residence I felt safe. No one knew I was there. Only the senior staff people were aware of my story; the other residents didn't know and wouldn't have cared. I knew I was not going to be hurt, and I knew just what was going to happen day after day; nothing was going to change. Life there was never exciting, but the sameness—and the fact that I could count on things being the same every day—in some ways felt like security to me. What's more, the FBI had its eye out for me, and you probably can't get more safe than that.

In fact, the FBI had me not under wraps exactly, but they definitely wanted me to lie low and get out of the spotlight of Cleveland—at least until the pretrial hearings were held and an indictment against Castro was handed down. They were concerned that if I went out in public, I would be recognized and possibly followed and my whereabouts discovered. That could mean a lot of people descending on me—journalists, TV people, whoever—and trying to get me to tell my story.

And the FBI didn't want anything to compromise the case before it got to trial. Neither did I, of course. The FBI also worried that a reporter or just anyone might snap a photo of me and sell it. That would blow my cover and my privacy— as well as being an awful thing for someone to do. So right from the start they requested that I talk to them before going too far away from the hospice. It wasn't really about asking permission but about keeping me safe and secure and as anonymous as possible for a while.

I certainly wasn't a prisoner at the hospice. I could come and go as I pleased, and I had the means to do it. A bank account had been set up for me to hold the money from the Cleveland Courage Fund, and I had a bankcard for paying bills and a debit card for going shopping. At first the FBI wasn't wild about me hitting the mall, and the truth is I didn't feel much like going anywhere; I was just too sick. But that wouldn't last, and I would eventually get the itch to go shopping again. I've always loved to shop.

MEANWHILE I could try to come to grips with my past and prepare to be part of the future. I had gone from hell into a hospital bed, and I still felt sick, but I knew I would need to think through a lot of things I had never thought through before, and I would need to plan a future that stretched before me as a blank space. For the first time in my life it was in my power to write what I wanted on that blank space, and having those six months in assisted living to do it was probably a good thing.

The facility I was sent to was definitely a weird place for me to be. Of course, it was licensed by the state and was regularly inspected, and everything about it was clean and well cared for by the family who operated it. Nothing weird in that sense. The family consisted of Rachel and her husband, their two young kids—a boy of about ten and a girl about seven—and Rachel's parents, who often helped out. But the place was called Happy Days Elderly Care, which really sums it up. Except for Rachel's family and the nurses who came in to work there during the day, everybody there was very old. There wasn't anybody under the age of about eighty-five. They were people at the end of their lives, too sick or too frail to completely take care of themselves, more or less waiting to die.

I was at a whole different point in life. I was thirty-two years old, with the worst of my life behind me, just now getting ready to begin living. At first, like the others, I was sick and weak, but unlike them, I was going to get better and move on. I probably stood out like a sore thumb to the elderly residents, if they noticed me at all, but to me, it was a lonely feeling and a little bit depressing to be in a place where people were dying around me. Eventually another young woman arrived, but by then I was at the end of my stay.

It was also depressing to feel as sick as I still felt at the beginning of my stay there. When I was discharged from Metro-Health I was able to get myself upright if I had to. But I was still taking a lot of medication—especially antibiotics. I don't remember the names, but I do remember that they made everything I tried to eat taste like metal, and they made me feel wobbly too.

In fact, for the first several weeks I was in hospice I was back and forth to the hospital pretty regularly. Almost as soon as I had settled in, I suffered another fever and got rushed back to emergency care, this time at Cleveland Clinic. There I was given another round of antibiotics intravenously and was sent back to the hospice with a Z-pak of more antibiotic doses. But I still couldn't tolerate food, I kept catching colds, and I was just plain sick all the time.

One day my fever hit 103, and I put in a frightened phone call to Lisa, the FBI agent who was working the case against Castro, and asked her to drive me to Cleveland Clinic. As we were leaving, one of the nurses at Happy Days called out to us, "Have them check her for C. diff." I had no idea what that was, but Lisa remembered the warning and told the doctors at the Clinic. They tested me and, sure enough, clostridium difficile was precisely what I had. C. diff, as it is called, is a bacterial infection that can inflame the colon and eventually kill you. You get it from unsanitary conditions—bad air, dirty water, food handled by unclean hands—exactly the kind of conditions I had lived in for eleven years in Castro's filthy house. That is almost certainly where and how I picked up the C. diff bug, and the heavy doses of antibiotics I had been getting since being rescued from the house didn't help because antibiotics often kill some of the normal, helpful bacteria in your gut while they're also destroying the bacteria they're meant to kill.

In fact, as it turns out, elderly people in hospitals or in long-term care facilities like Happy Days are the people who most commonly get C. diff. It's why the nurse at Happy Days knew about it, and I'm glad she did, because the doctors at Cleveland Clinic told me that my case was pretty far gone. They said if I had been held in Castro's house much longer, I surely would have died. As it was, I was hospitalized at Cleveland Clinic for two whole weeks after my diagnosis, and for much of that time I sure felt like I was going to die. But I just kept saying to myself, *I'm not going to die today, and I'm not going to die tomorrow.* I kept telling myself that the reason I had gotten out of the house before the C. diff killed me was the same reason I would get past the C. diff. To me, it was clear that there was something I had to do in life, and I was surviving whatever I came up against so I could get it done.

After two weeks in Cleveland Clinic I went back "home" to the assisted-living facility. I was still very, very weak. I really didn't have the strength to take care of myself. I felt lightheaded, couldn't take a shower unaided, and had to be fed. Rachel basically spooned some sort of strained porridge into me. Later I would realize that one reason she did that was because of the television reports suggesting that I was retarded and couldn't take care of myself. The day after I found that out, I went into the kitchen and started to cook for myself. And I mean I cooked up a storm—chili, my famous garlic cheesy mashed potatoes, steaks, cakes, cookies. I figured it was time I made it clear that I was not at all retarded and could take care of myself just fine, thank you very much. But that was later. For the moment I was just not yet ready.

Being sick and weak made my loneliness and depression even worse. Surrounded by folks who were almost certainly never going to leave this place alive, I struggled to get through my weakness so I could move on.

I felt I needed privacy for my struggle, and there just wasn't any. Yes, I had my own very pleasant room with two beds and a private bathroom. I used one of the beds to line up a whole "zoo" of the stuffed animals that had come from well-wishers, and I decorated one whole wall with all the cards I had received in the hospital. The room had a window as well, with a view out to a spacious green lawn, trees, and a pond. But there was a sort of "open-door policy" at the assisted-living facility, and other residents thought nothing of wandering in on foot or in their wheelchairs to have a look around. They probably didn't mean to be nosy, but I was at a point in my life when I very much wanted my own space. I needed boundaries, and I needed respect, and not having either made me anxious and very, very uncomfortable.

In addition, I was still answering questions from the FBI agents and my lawyer, still dredging up the awful things that had happened in Castro's house as evidence for the case they were bringing against him. I knew it was important to tell the whole story, but it was hard to go through it all again.

So in those first weeks at Happy Days my days were not terribly happy. Just about everything seemed strange to me.

Just about everything made me anxious. I was at the start of a difficult, day-by-day process of trying to understand that what I had gone through was not my fault and did not define me. There was a lot to think about, and for that I needed space as well as time.

What's more, interacting with other human beings just did not come easy to me in those early weeks of freedom. The last eleven years and much of my life before that had made me believe that human beings were the worst creatures on earth, that they were abusive, bullying, and cruel— the only animals capable of evil for its own sake. I still very nearly shuddered every time I laid eyes on any man at all, but trying to trust anyone—man or woman—was hard to do.

There were at least ten other residents in the hospice facility, some of whom shared rooms, and there was a sitting area and dining area for all. I sometimes sat with the others on the comfortable sofa to watch television, but that set was really too small for my struggling eyes, so I bought my own, which Rachel's husband hooked up for me. At mealtimes in the dining area I found I just did not care much for the food Rachel and her husband prepared, although I knew I needed to eat what I could. It wasn't until I started cooking for myself that I began to put some meat on my bones. Still, I pretty much stuck to my room. I wasn't dealing with other people to any great extent.

Slowly, slowly, I began to feel stronger and better. One day I felt good enough to take my clothes to the laundry room to run them through the washing machine. That's how

I met Dorothy, one of the oldest of the residents. Her room was nearby, and I heard people singing hymns in there. So I peeked in, and two younger women, who turned out to be her daughters, said, "Come on in and sing with us." I did. It was the start of a true friendship.

Unlike many of the residents, Dorothy was cheerful and kind. She never had a bad word to say about anyone; I guess that's why I felt peaceful when I was with her. She loved having visitors in her room. When you walked in, her face would light up in a big, bright smile.

She was quite old, with longish, wispy white hair and pale blue eyes. And she was mostly bedridden, although occasionally they put her in the wheelchair and rolled her out of her room so she could get her hair shampooed, or they would bring her into the sitting area and she would sit there and say, "How's everybody doing?" She had some form of dementia, so she couldn't remember things. In fact, each time her daughters showed up, they had to tell her who they were.

She didn't much remember my name either, but she always seemed glad to see me. And I felt totally comfortable with her—a feeling I didn't get elsewhere or with others in the hospice. When we first started talking she asked me why I was there, and I told her I was very sick. At the time the doctors actually still thought I might die, and I told her that.

"Honey, you're too young to die," she said. "You got all your life to live." She made me believe it too.

The daughters were wonderful women, just as sweet as their mother and good daughters as well. They visited their mother regularly, and their visits always made the whole place brighter and turned up the spirits of all the residents and staff in their orbit. They sang with their mother on just about every visit, and I was always invited, so there we would be—Dorothy, her daughters, and me, belting out hymn after hymn about the goodness of the Lord.

One day Dorothy was talking to me about her daughters, telling me how sweet it was of them to come and visit "a little old lady like me." Then she turned to me and said, "You're kind of like my daughter too." I smiled. "Thank you," I said. Kind and loving, Dorothy seemed to me a far cry from my real mother.

I made another friend at the hospice too: Anita. She wasn't a resident there. At the time she was a friend of Rachel's who just enjoyed visiting, and she was very sweet. A retired flight attendant, which I thought was so cool, Anita had no children of her own, but she treated each of us like a daughter or son. She loved everybody, and she too was a special friend of Dorothy's. Once I was able to leave the facility for brief outings, Anita and I often went out for the evening. We would go to a restaurant or club and have a margarita or two, maybe do some dancing, and talk about our lives. She would tell me about some of the famous people she had met when she was flying, and we both loved animals, and we would just chill. I think Anita was probably in her sixties at that time, but she behaved like someone my age. She was just fun to be with. An evening out with Anita made me feel relaxed and at ease when I got back to the hospice, always

just before the curfew. It washed away the depression of being around people dying. She warmed my heart, and I found
her inspiring.

She also helped me get through the C. diff, which took a
long time. Basically, the doctors were medicating me for the
pain while they tried different cures for the condition. It took
a while to identify the right medication for me, and Anita
helped me through that struggle. She stood by my side when
I needed her the most. She's one of the friends who never
walked away. I found her uplifting in every way. I still do.

I also got to know one of Anita's close friends, Erna, who
sometimes came along with her to visit. The two of them
together were a real hoot. They were about the same age,
but they acted like goofy teenagers when they were together.
Being around the two of them was like a shot of energy flavored with joy.

And I got friendly with Rachel's two kids. They were both
blonde and blue-eyed and very cute. I called them the little
marshmallows—the boy was Marshmallow One, and the girl
was Marshmallow Two. The little girl was pretty shy, but she
brought her hamster over to "introduce" him to me, and she
let me hold him. I was terrified I was going to drop him; he
was absolutely wild and frisky and clearly just wanted to be
out of my hand. He was the first hamster I ever knew, but by
no means the last.

As soon as I felt well enough, I headed outdoors. In fact, I spent a lot of time outdoors that summer. As it always does, being in nature brought me peace. The pond on the property was big and very beautiful. A dirt track circled it all the way around. So as the medication kicked in and the C. diff started to get kicked out, and as I grew stronger and healthier, I started walking around the pond.

The fresh air was a relief after the gloomy atmosphere in the hospice residence. The place just felt dark, as if death were all around me. So being outside, in nature, where everything was alive, was a good antidote to that.

The pond was about a quarter of a mile around, and I worked my way up to walking around it multiple times a day. Then, when I got even stronger, I began running around the pond. I had been a pretty strong runner when I was a kid. I was always short in stature, of course, with short legs, so when I started running, the kids at school called me Minnie Mouse. But my short legs could certainly move, and I got to be pretty fast. At thirty-two, still not in the best of health and with nerve damage in both legs as a result of torture, I wasn't so fast anymore, but I was glad to find I could still run. Rachel's husband was working outside and watched me run around the pond that first day, when I thought I was just jogging at a modest pace.

"Do you have fire on those shoes?" he shouted as I came around the track. "You went around that pond so fast! You can't be too sick after all if you can run that fast."

I may have been propelled by adrenaline. After eleven years of being restrained, unable to move and locked indoors, just to be outside, moving, and feeling the wind on my face was like having a motor pushing me forward. No wonder I went around again—and again and again. Six times around the pond: running made me feel alive.

But then there were the geese. We have huge populations of Canada geese in my part of the country—Ohio and all the Great Lakes area—and the pond in Hinckley seemed to be a favorite habitat for a sizeable flock of them. The part of the track that the geese crossed to get into the pond could be difficult to navigate: walking or running, I had to step carefully to avoid the slippery droppings the geese left behind or, often enough, to avoid actually running into one of the flock. I guess they felt the same way about me because sometimes they would run after me to chase me off their territory. I began to wonder if my jogging had become a game to them. They would suddenly dart out from behind a group of pine trees they had been hiding behind and lunge at me as I ran past. I kept an eye out for them, but the grass was high around the pond, so I couldn't always see them.

One of the staff members at Happy Days was worried about me. "Hey," she said one day, pointing to the supply of canes and walking sticks available in the residence, "take one of these sticks out there for protection, because one of these days those geese are going to get you!" I thanked her but explained that I wouldn't be comfortable running with a stick in my hands. I think I also figured I could always outrun a bunch of geese. So off I went.

It was a warm summer day. The pond looked calm, the tree foliage was still the bright-green color of high summer, and the running felt good. My body had begun loosening up, and I could kind of feel that my muscles, so long unused, were stretching out and getting into action again.

I noticed some movement in the pond and looked over to see small fish jumping in and out of the water. Because I was watching the fish, however, I did *not* see the geese emerging from the brush. Grass is the standard favorite diet of geese, but they also eat fish when they can get it, and suddenly I was in the way of their headlong rush for the meal that was just then flipping in and out of the pond. I thought I was outrunning the flock when I caught sight of a large female goose with four or five babies behind her, all heading straight for the pond. One thing I know is true for just about all animals on earth: you don't want to get between a mama and her babies—not between a lion and her cubs, not between an elephant and her calf, not between a goose and her goslings, because if and when mama senses you're going to hurt her babies, she is going to do anything necessary to stop you. This mama was coming right at me with a pretty unpleasant look in her eye, so I took a flying leap to avoid her, slipped, and splashed right into the pond.

The problem was I couldn't swim. Making the problem worse: I panicked. The pond was deeper than I ever thought, and I started flailing to stay above the surface. Fortunately, I grabbed hold of a chunk of grass growing at the edge of the pond and got stable. Then I began to yell like crazy. Marshmallow One, Rachel's young son, heard me and yelled for his parents, and they hauled me out of there.

After that, I carried the cane when I jogged.

Running wasn't my only form of exercise or recreation. I also got into boxing in a fairly big way. Correction: I got *back* into boxing.

It's a sport I had loved since I was a little girl. I had been a big fan of Manny Pacquiao, one of the greatest, most famous, winningest boxers of all time, and I had followed his career and the sport itself as best I could. I also liked to punch. Not people and not to do harm, but I did punch out of anger. As a little girl, whenever anyone in the family abused me, I would go upstairs and start punching my pillow. In fact, along with writing in my journal, boxing was my go-to way to "express" my anger and fear and unhappiness as I was growing up.

But of course, I hadn't been able to follow boxing or think about it for eleven years. I guess I maybe mentioned Manny Pacquiao once in Castro's hearing.

"Pacquiao?" Castro said. "That guy is dead!" Only, of course, Castro didn't call Pacquiao a "guy"—he used some ugly racist or ethnic slur. I believed him, though, and I felt very sad about it, but as I learned later, it was a total lie. Castro was just a man who couldn't bear to see anyone love anything. He figured it would hurt me to be told that Pacquiao was dead, and any way he could hurt me, he would.

But almost by accident I found my way back to doing boxing. My shopping itch had kicked in, and because I hadn't been anywhere near a store for eleven years, I was eager to see what was available and to just have the chance to buy something frivolous if I wanted to. The news about the three of us and our ordeal and our rescue had died down a lot. Our faces and names were no longer plastered all over the papers and television. So I figured it was time to ask Rachel to check with the FBI and see about taking me shopping.

She did and was told the Bureau would still prefer if I waited a bit. The agents were still building their case against Castro, and the FBI was still worried that if I went out in public, I would be recognized and that someone or something might somehow slip through the net to compromise the case. So I tried to be patient, but I really was becoming very eager to get out into the world, so to speak. This was beginning to feel like another kind of captivity, and I was itching to spread my wings.

But finally the FBI said okay, and off we went to one of those huge, all-purpose stores that seemed to me more like a warehouse than a store. I was amazed at the variety of things available and at the look of the products. Light bulbs, headsets, backpacks: even standard items looked fresh and different to me. The thing that caught my eye was a punching bag, the kind you could attach to the ceiling and just bat away at endlessly. Rachel vetoed that one because it would need to be attached to a stud beam or it could wreck the ceiling and anyone standing under it, and fooling around with a stud beam was too serious a change. Instead, we went for the free-standing punching bag in which you fill the base with sand. I had had something like it when I was a kid and had loved it, so I was thrilled to get this one. I got a pair of boxing gloves as well.

We took it all home and set up the punching bag outside. I put on the gloves, stood in front of the bag, stared at it for a bit, then I punched it as hard as I could—so hard that I pounded it right over onto the ground.

"What were you thinking," Rachel asked me, "when you landed that punch?"

"Honey," I answered, "I was just imagining his face right there." Rachel knew I meant Ariel Castro's face. Because he had yet to be tried, he was still presumed innocent in the eyes of the law. But not in my eyes, of course; I knew his guilt firsthand. Just the thought of him filled me with enough anger and hatred to knock a four-hundred-pound bag to the ground so hard that it very nearly broke the spring action of the stem.

After that, I used the punching bag pretty regularly about every three days—not just to hit but to stay in shape. It did make me feel good, and it did help build my strength.

If I thought the store that Rachel and I went to was new and different, it was minor compared to the other changes I was seeing and hearing on television and all around me. I had missed a lot. In the time I was "away," the country had gone to war, the internet had exploded, there had been a global financial crisis, we had elected the first African American president, and the planet had seen devastating hurricanes and earthquakes. I had been pretty much unaware of it all.

The music I was hearing was totally different too—and nowhere near as good, in my view, as the music of the eighties and nineties. The new stuff didn't seem to mean anything, and it all sounded the same to me. I still feel that way: give me the music of the eighties and nineties any day. Anyway, I think my favorite piece of music will always be Celine Dion singing "My Heart Will Go On." That's a song from the nineties that meant so much to me during my captivity and ever since. In fact, one of the great experiences of my life was getting the chance to meet Celine Dion, nearly a year after my time in the hospice, and to tell her how important her song and her voice were in my life.

But if the music confused me, what rocked me most of all was the technology: iPhones, tablets, YouTube, and something called Facebook. The change in the way people communicated and entertained themselves was mind-boggling.

I do not remember who gave me my first cell phone. It was an iPhone 5, and it didn't take long for me to want to throw it against the wall. I had absolutely no idea what I was doing and could not even figure out how to turn it on. I had to ask the FBI to let me go to the store and get a manual that I could understand, and then I still couldn't figure it out.

True, this was fairly early on at Happy Days, so I was still pretty sick and disoriented. I wasn't functioning all that well. But I forced myself through that manual, and every time I thought I had the thing licked, I turned out to be wrong. *Why is this so complicated?* I wondered. *Why can't I get this?*

For once, I was glad people found it normal to wander into my room, because one day in comes Marshmallow Two who sees me struggling with the iPhone. At seven years of age, she of course knew exactly how to use it, and she was patient enough to teach me. She also introduced me to Facebook, which I thought at first was maybe a little too mature for a seven-year-old. I was actually kind of stunned at the negativity I saw there—I still am—but I also saw how useful it could be as a way to connect privately with a circle of friends. And I certainly saw the internet as a whole—the worldwide web—as a gateway into information and an opportunity to connect with others and expand your life.

I was beginning to think about that very thing—expanding my life. I thought about getting a place of my own, a small apartment maybe. I remember mentioning it once to Dorothy, and she encouraged me to do it.

But before I could focus on that, there was something I had to do.

ON JUNE 7, 2013, Castro had been officially charged with several crimes. Five of the charges were for aggravated murder for having terminated my five pregnancies. He was charged July 12 for more crimes: kidnapping, rape, gross sexual imposition, felonious assault, child endangerment, and more—a total of 977 charges. He pleaded guilty on July 26 in a plea bargain that would sentence him to consecutive life sentences plus a thousand years in prison without the possibility of parole. His house would also be demolished. A sentencing hearing was scheduled for August 1.

I got a call from the office of the trial judge asking if I wanted to make a statement at the hearing. I didn't have to appear in person, the judge assured me; I could have my lawyer read whatever I wrote. Amanda and Gina were not planning to appear; family members would read their statements for them. That was their decision, and I respect it. For me, with no family to speak for me anyway, there was no way I was not going to appear in court, face my tormentor, and say my piece.

I wrote the statement, and when the day came, I went to the courthouse, entered the courtroom, and stood before the judge. On one side of me was my lawyer; on the other side was Lisa, the FBI agent who knew the case so well and had become a friend. At moments as I spoke I felt a reassuring hand on my shoulder from each one of them. I know I was trembling. In the course of saying what I had come there to say, I had to bite back the tears that threatened to muffle my words. I was in a court of law, the home of justice, and I was not going to let anything keep me from saying every word clearly. Nothing would stop me from being heard and understood. This is what I told the judge and the world:

Good afternoon. My name is Michelle Knight. And I would like to tell you what this was like for me.

I missed my son every day. I wondered if I was ever going to see him again. He was only two and a half years old when I was taken. I look inside my heart and I see my son. I cried every night. I was so alone. I worried about what would happen to me and the other girls every day.

Days never got shorter. Days turned into nights. Nights turned into days. The years turned into eternity.

I knew nobody cared about me. He told me that my family didn't care even on holidays. Christmas was the most traumatic day because I never got to spend it with my son. Nobody should ever have to go through what I went through, not even one's worst enemy.

Gina was my teammate. She never let me fall. I never let her fall. She nursed me back to health when I was dying from his abuse. My friendship with her is the only thing that was good out of this situation. We said we would someday make it out alive, and we did.

Ariel Castro, I remember all the times that you came home talking about what everybody else did wrong and act like you wasn't doing the same thing.

You said, at least I didn't kill you. For you took eleven years of my life away, and I have got it back. I spent eleven years in hell, and now your hell is just beginning. I will overcome all this that happened, but you will face hell for eternity.

From this moment on, I will not let you define me or affect who I am. You will live—I will live on. You will die a little every day.

As you think about the eleven years and atrocities you inflicted on us, what does God think of you hypocritically going to church every Sunday, coming home to torture us? The death penalty would be so much easier. You don't deserve that. You deserve to spend life in prison. I can forgive you, but I will never forget. With the guidance of God, I will prevail and help others that suffered at the hands of others.

Writing this statement gave me the strength to be a stronger woman, and I know that there's good— there is more good than evil.

I know that there is a lot of people going through hard times, but we need to reach out a hand and hold them and let them know that they're being heard.

After eleven years, I am finally being heard, and it's liberating.

Thank you, all. I love you. God bless you.

Six days later I was present when the house on Seymour Avenue, the house in which I had been imprisoned and tortured, was demolished. I released a bunch of yellow balloons into the air, and in a statement I gave to the reporters I said the balloons "represent all the millions of children that were never found and the ones that passed away that were never heard." I said I hoped that God would give "strength and power to all missing people."

"They are caterpillars," I said, "waiting to turn into butterflies. They are never forgotten, they are loved."

Then I watched as Gina's aunt climbed up into the cab of the wrecking crane and powered the first smash of the house. I didn't stay much past that. With the cameras and reporters and the noise of destruction, it all seemed chaotic to me. The total demolition took more than an hour, and I'm told that toward the end, church bells rang out.

A FEW DAYS AFTER that, my lawyer phoned and asked if I would be interested in writing a book about what had happened to me. She had been contacted by a literary agency—I barely knew what that was—and they were interested in helping me tell my story. They thought it was an important story and that it could help others.

I pretty much dismissed the idea. Writing a book seemed crazy to me. Yes, I loved to write, but I wrote for myself. I wrote to get things down on paper, to clarify what I was thinking and feeling. It was a way of talking to myself, to my son, to God. A book was something else altogether.

But my lawyer and the agent asked me to think about it, so I did. Long and hard. I thought about missing children all over the world and their parents. I thought about abused kids who never got the help they should be getting. *I've been there*, I thought. *I know how you feel. You feel hopeless, like there's nothing left. But it isn't true. You can overcome this. You can build a life. You can find happiness. I know it's possible.*

I guess that's when I realized that maybe I should write a book after all. I had said in my statement to the judge that I wanted to help those who suffered at the hands of others. Maybe this was a way to do that. A way to begin, anyway.

THERE WERE two important deaths that September. Late in the evening of September 3 I got a phone call from Gina telling me she had just heard on the news that Castro had killed himself in his prison cell. The idea that suddenly he could be dead blew my mind. I didn't get how it could've happened, though: Wasn't he on suicide watch or something? Weren't the authorities looking out for something like that?

The next morning Rachel came into my room and sat down on the second bed. "I don't know if you've heard the news," she said. I told her I had. "How do you feel about it?" she asked me. "Are you okay?"

"'Feel'?" I said. "I can't feel anything for someone who hurt me so much. I guess I am sorry for his family that he hurt them one more time, but I am certainly not sad."

I asked to be left alone for a while, and I just sat there and wept as I processed the information. This monster had been in prison for about a month; I had survived his prison for eleven years. A news report said he had complained a few days earlier that the guards were harassing him. "I don't know if I can take this neglect anymore, and the way I'm being treated," he wrote in his journal. I only wished he had been forced to take it much longer. He had taken the selfish way out, I thought. I was angry he had escaped the punishment he deserved; his sentence was nowhere near as harsh as the one he had imposed on me, Amanda, and Gina.

Not long afterward Dorothy died in her sleep. That was a real loss—my one true friend in the assisted-living facility and the brightest spot in my world at the time. I mourned her death.

Meanwhile summer was fading fast. My health was definitely improving, and I was beginning to think more and more that I should start figuring out my next step. I wanted to leave, but I was in no way clear about where to go and what to do. I still wasn't comfortable in the hospice, even though Rachel had taken in some younger women with various issues. They were slightly closer to my age anyway.

I got to be friendly with a couple of the young women; one was afraid of everything while another fantasized about marrying Justin Bieber. They had plenty of insecurities. They felt worthless, were upset about the way they looked, and couldn't see their own beauty or inner value or understand that what counted was who they were inside and what they chose to make of their lives.

I recognized those insecurities. I had been told for most of my life that I was a nobody, and I had been treated like a nobody as well. But I was now beginning to see that, having survived what I survived, I had real strength. I was beginning to think I needed to be confident about that strength. Mostly, I was beginning to see that I could not let my past define me. I wasn't "what had happened to me." I was me, a human being with feelings and gifts and qualities that had been tested in a way few people get tested. I was me, and I could control my own destiny. I tried to tell that to these women. I wanted them to know that the lives stretching ahead of them were blank canvases and that it was up to them to draw the picture they wanted their lives to be. The same was true of me. Working through these insecurities together, these women and I formed a real connection, and in trying to convince them that their lives were in their hands, I reminded myself that the same was true of me. I began to feel that it was time for me to take the next step, to move on in my life. At that moment the next step meant a place where I could feel okay, a place with privacy, a place of my own. I felt I was ready.

Then Lisa, my favorite FBI agent, came out to the hospice and told me they had found out about Joey.

LISA AND I went into my room, and she closed the door. I was terrified. She tried to break it to me gently, but the news was that the FBI had tracked down the family who had adopted Joey about nine years before, when he was four, and that the family did not want their identity or their whereabouts known.

Was I glad to know he was safe? More than you can imagine. Glad and grateful above everything else. Since the day I went into Castro's house, I had no idea where my boy was or what was happening to him, no way of knowing if he was still in foster care, nothing but a mother's prayer and hope that he was alive and well somewhere. That prayer was answered—Joey was alive and safe. My hope was fulfilled. I breathed a great sigh of relief.

And although I tried to understand the adoptive family's insistence on keeping their identity a secret, it frightened and upset me something fierce at the same time. I had seen the craziness with the media that had accompanied our rescue, Castro's trial, the house demolition, and his suicide, and I understood that even a hint of that kind of publicity could disrupt or destroy a family's tranquility. I also realized that it could be extremely confusing and unsettling for Joey. I couldn't blame his new family for wanting to stay far away from what I knew could be a kind of circus atmosphere.

But did that mean there was no way I would ever see or connect with my son again? I could feel my heart tearing apart at the thought. My son had been the center of my life since his birth. Not a day had passed when I did not think about him, worry about him, pray for his well-being. Nothing would ever change that, and learning that he would remain out of my life—maybe forever—just broke me. I didn't think I could bear it.

A day went by. Two days. I called Lisa and asked her to come to the hospice again. I wanted her to let the family know that what I wanted was not to take Joey away from them—I knew that wouldn't be right for any of us—but just for him to know that I never ran out on him, that he was never ever abandoned by me, his birth mother, but just that terrible things took over my life and kept me from him. I also wanted him to know that I would love to connect with him one day, on his terms, at his request. I asked Lisa to tell all that to his new family.

What Lisa was able to arrange was for me to write a letter to Joey's adoptive parents. I wrote it blind—I had no idea who they were, what they looked like, where they were, what they did for a living, what they did for fun, or anything about them—and it would be the FBI who arranged for the letter to be "delivered."

In the letter I thanked the adoptive parents for their care of my son, told them so many of the things I wondered about him—his likes and dislikes, his friends, his favorite sports, his personality—and asked if they would be so kind as to send me a photo.

They did better than that. They sent me several photos showing Joey at different ages and at different stages of development. It was generous of them, and I respect their request that I keep the photos to myself and show them to no one else. But I look at them daily. It gives me joy to see myself within my boy, and of course, I continue to yearn to meet him again one day.

Still, finding out what I now knew about Joey did put an end to the most nagging questions about his life and his well-being. I now at least knew for certain that he was alive and well and part of a family who clearly loved him and was concerned about him. Perhaps one day God will make it possible for me to get the answers to all my questions from Joey himself.

In the meantime it really was time for me to put the hospice and assisted living behind me. I began to scour the real estate offerings and look at apartments for rent in downtown Cleveland. I was ready to take the next step.

But first I had agreed to go on nationwide television and tell the story of my captivity and torture to millions of viewers.

CHAPTER FOUR

On My Own — and in Search of Friends

I still have my fears, but I don't let them determine how I live my life . . .

I HAD NOT EVEN heard of Dr. Phil McGraw before I was kidnapped. After several years in Castro's house, when the three of us were able to watch television, I saw snippets of some of his shows—a few minutes here and a few minutes there—as long as they didn't have any African Americans on them. Castro was a bigot who hated all people of color and would punish us if we watched any TV show with African Americans.

But at least I knew *about* Dr. Phil when my lawyer told me about the request to go on the show for a one-on-one interview about what I had gone through. I thought hard about it. I knew that describing my experience would be tough, but I always believed mine was a story that had to be told. This was another way to do it, different from reporters writing down what you say and different too from writing a book. All I had to do was answer questions. I said yes.

The interview was to take place in California—in a quiet, secluded location where I would feel protected. As everybody knows, Dr. Phil is a big man with a deep voice and a forthright manner. I felt like an ant next to him. I was still uneasy around men, but he is such a kind and reassuring guy that he put me at ease.

The taping took place over a couple of days in October. The set was a living room. I settled myself cross-legged on the sofa while Dr. Phil sat opposite me in a chair. Of course I was nervous at first. He asked question after question. He asked softly. He reacted quietly but with feeling. Talking to him got easier with each question. I felt okay—I felt safe—about sharing my story with him.

We talked first about Castro's abduction of me, about being chained to that pole in the filthy basement of the house, about being tied up like a fish and hung like a hammock by an orange extension cord. We talked about how I realized, even in those first months of captivity, that because I knew his name and his face, Castro could never let me go free without ending up in prison himself. After a time we talked about when first Gina and then Amanda arrived in the house, about the growing bond between Gina and me, and about how Castro always singled me out for the worst beatings—as we all knew, because I refused to break no matter what he did.

Those two days of the interview were hard going, as I had expected they would be, but I felt good to have done it. Dr. Phil said something afterward that meant a lot to me. "I started this by thinking that I was sitting down with a brave and courageous young woman," he said. "And after spending these few days with you here, I now know that brave and courageous are not big enough words to describe you." His words made me feel almost his size. In turn, I had come to feel that he really cared about my life and where I was going with it. When he told me I could call him any time, I believed him. It was real.

The interview was televised over two days too. The first hour, shown on Tuesday, November 5, was the part about

57

my abduction and the years before Gina and Amanda. The second part was on Wednesday, November 6, about relationships among the three of us and how I was singled out for brutality because I was unbreakable. That Saturday, November 9, both parts were rebroadcast as a two-hour special. The audience for these shows was huge all over the country but especially in northeast Ohio. It meant that just as I got ready to move into my new apartment and start trying to live a normal life, there was no way I could escape celebrity.

Mine was a funny kind of celebrity too. I hadn't achieved something special through talent and hard work. I'm no movie star, and as for athletic ability, I'm not exactly LeBron James. That's not the kind of celebrity I am. I'm known for having survived something horrible, for having been terrorized by a human monster and having refused to become a victim. Now I was trying to reclaim my life, but feeling people staring at me every time I walked outside wasn't helping. In fact, it was scaring me.

When I had first begun looking at apartments, a chief concern was security. That meant many different things to me. First, I wanted to be in a lively neighborhood where there were lots of people around, plenty of activity, and plenty of good lighting. Shadows and empty spaces were a turnoff. I also decided I would look mostly at recently constructed buildings that would have lots of up-to-date features and amenities. I figured that such buildings would also have the latest security measures.

What actually first attracted me to the building I would eventually move into was that it was in a complex filled with athletes. A number of players on Cleveland's professional baseball, football, and basketball teams had apartments there, and the building management was very concerned with protecting their privacy and keeping any "fans" out of range of the tenants and off the premises. That meant heavy security: key fobs for entry, a twenty-four-hour guard in the lobby of the building, cameras tracking traffic coming in and going out. That was a real attraction, and when I was shown the apartment—a one-bedroom with a full living room and a gorgeous country-style kitchen—I decided this was home. I signed a one-year lease, packed up my few belongings, and moved in—just in time for Thanksgiving.

I still needed help to furnish and decorate the apartment, and you know who provided that help? Dr. Phil. He kind of took me shopping—well, not in person, which isn't possible when you run a daily television show—but he arranged it all. He sent two assistants—blonde, pretty, unbelievably efficient—to help me get it done. And believe me, if you're an assistant for Dr. Phil, you really know how to get things done. They hired a car service, and off we went, spending hours in Macy's and Value City buying furniture, pots and pans, even new clothes—absolutely every last possible thing a person could need. A key goal was to make sure things matched— the dining room furniture and the living room furniture and the bedroom set too. I didn't want anything to be "out of order." And nothing was. Dr. Phil asked me to send photos of "your gorgeous new apartment," which of course I did. I will always be grateful to him for that boost to help me start a new life.

I NEEDED A BOOST. Much as I had craved being downtown and on my own, neither was easy. I lacked what people call a "support group," which I've always thought was just another term for friends and family. I knew there was no support possible from my family, but as I was winding down my time at the assisted-living facility, I did reach out to some old friends from my childhood.

In particular, I wanted to reconnect with the person I thought of as my best friend from high school. When I started looking for a place to live, she offered space in her apartment. It made sense. She was a single mom at the time, and the way she put it, sharing a place would work for both of us. "I could use some help with the rent," she said, "and it would give you a place for yourself and your things while you look for a permanent home." It sounded to me like a good deal, and what could be easier than striking a deal with someone you've known since you were a kid in high school?

But it didn't work out. It seemed to me that she was only interested in getting money to pay the rent, and the whole thing ended badly. Some people come into your life as a lesson. My "bestie" from high school was a lesson that you can't trust someone just because you were kids together.

My so-called cousin was another lesson. She wanted to write her own book about "our" family. But rather than help, I got the definite impression that she was only interested in my celebrity status. I disconnected that family "connection" pretty quickly.

I saw both these failures as betrayals. It's a harsh word, but that's how I felt. How can you not think that an old friend and a cousin will be anything other than glad to help in your time of need? Where else should you turn when you need a lift up—especially when you're just barely holding yourself together after hitting rock bottom? Both experiences felt like blows, and I grew more determined than ever to break with everything in my past and find a new way of life peopled with new friends.

The complex that included my building had just about everything anyone needed: restaurants, gyms, even a hair salon. You almost never had to leave the complex at all, but if you did, there were all sorts of stores and markets right in the neighborhood within easy walking distance. Because I couldn't drive and was still too frightened to get into a taxi, that was certainly useful.

I remember opening the door that first day after everything had been delivered. I stood looking at my shiny furniture, smelling that new couch smell. I was so excited to have a place of my own. I had done it! I had the privacy I craved. I didn't have to answer to anyone or defer to anyone. There was no one to tell me what to do or when to do it, no one wandering into my space as if they owned it, no one commenting on my habits or activities, no one talking to me or at me for any reason.

And as soon as I moved in, I was terrified. I had finally gotten my wish to be alone, and what I felt was lonely. I tried to say "hi" to everybody I passed in the building or around the complex—a lot of people must have thought I was kind of kooky.

I began to realize that freedom was a funny thing. I was free in the sense that I was away from the horrors of Castro's house and the abuse of my family. And I was free to choose where and how I would live. I could do anything I was capable of—take a walk, learn to fly, get a pet, sing, dance, vote. But I couldn't walk out on the street without being recognized.

People stared. Once, when I was first taken to shop for clothes, I noticed another shopper, a woman, snapping photos of me with her phone while I was in the changing room. I asked her, politely, to please stop.

"This is a public area," she said. "You can't tell me what to do."

"What would you think," I asked her, "if someone took pictures of you while you were trying on clothes?"

"I don't care what people think of me," she said. I had to get the store manager over, and she asked the woman to leave. It certainly soured my shopping experience.

But it was my first lesson—and far from the last—that if you are in the public eye, people sometimes think they own you or that you owe them something. I guess with my story having become national news—even international news—I couldn't expect complete privacy. But every human being needs space to breathe. When I felt cameras closing in on me, it was almost like being in captivity all over again. And it was scary.

In the end, that became true even of the well-wishers who came up to me when I just went outside for a bit to stretch my legs on a walk around the neighborhood.

"I just want to tell you how happy I am that you were found," people would say. Or they would come up to me and tell me I was an "inspiration" to them. Many told me they prayed for me. I was grateful for the kind feelings. Their good wishes meant a lot to me. Still, knowing that people are looking at you all the time can put an awful lot of pressure on what you were hoping would be a casual walk outside. The attention can also make you feel vulnerable, and that reinforced my own fear of ever leaving the safe boundaries of the complex.

What I hadn't yet learned were the responsibilities of being free—the responsibility to confront reality, to believe in something other than evil, to teach myself how to take toxic people out of my life and put positive people back in. Developing that internal guidance system would take time.

So at first, mostly, I stayed home. In the apartment I unwrapped new art supplies I had bought and took pleasure in drawing and painting. Or I wrote in my new pink journal. When I felt myself going stir-crazy, I would go out to one of the restaurants in the complex, have a meal and a couple of drinks, and just come home.

I started a Facebook page—photo, profile, the whole thing. It exploded. Hundreds of people found me every day, added me as a friend, and sent me messages of encouragement. Facebook didn't scare me. The people contacting me on Facebook were from somewhere else; they existed in cyberspace, not on the street where I walked. There was enough distance between us that I didn't feel threatened.

The month I moved into the apartment was the same month we signed the contract to write the book that would become *Finding Me*. I didn't know where or how to begin, but the publisher assigned a professional editor to work with me. That meant long talks on the phone and lots of emails back and forth—and lots of thinking about how to relate what had happened to me over the eleven years of captivity. The pain of those years was never far beneath the surface, and focusing on them the way writing a book makes you focus brought it back pretty intensely. I found myself taking sips of wine during the day, at home, instead of waiting to go out to a restaurant. It numbed the pain just a bit, just enough, I thought, to get through the day. Temporary numbness, that was all.

I felt I needed a new focus and decided to get a job. But everywhere I tried, I was told my "fame" would be a distraction. Like the woman in the clothing shop, people would try to take my photo or would ask for selfies, and no work would get done. Potential employers were kind about the rejections, but they rejected me just the same.

Instead, I started volunteering at a no-kill animal shelter. Even there my celebrity was something of a handicap. But I was happy if I could just spend some time in the back of the shelter shampooing the dogs, clipping their nails, and taking care of them where I didn't have to be seen.

I decided to take cooking classes. I love to cook. I love doing artsy things with food. I like making flowers out of onions, and I love creating tomato swirls and turning curly fries into snakes. Brandt Evans is a famous chef in Cleveland, and when he heard me say in a television interview that I loved to cook, he invited me to take his class.

I loved what I was learning there, but some of the other students made me uncomfortable. A couple of them couldn't stop asking me really personal questions about my ordeal in Castro's house. To say the least, this broke my concentration and distracted me from the work we were all trying to do. In addition, I was still allergic to many of the ingredients—mustard, for example, and even salt—so that I often felt nauseous in class. Food smells could sometimes make me sick as well; the smell of beans, rice, and meat mixed with certain spices brought back bad memories and could get me coughing to the point that I would actually throw up. And then being pestered over and over again by a couple of fellow students about things I wanted to forget didn't help. It was all just another reminder that trying to be a normal person living a normal life was out of reach—for the moment anyway. Reluctantly, and always grateful to Brandt, I quit the cooking class, deciding I would just cook at home.

Besides the allergies, I still confronted terrible phobias that Castro had drilled into me. The reaction to certain food smells was bad enough. But I was also terrified of motorcycle helmets because Castro had used one to limit my sight and my movement. And I was horribly afraid of cloth napkins. That whole first year after my rescue, whenever I would go to a nice restaurant, I would have to ask for a paper napkin instead of the cloth one. Cloth was what Castro would shove into my mouth so I couldn't scream whenever he had people over to his house. One time he shoved a cloth napkin so far down the back of my mouth and into my throat that I could barely breathe. I began weeping, and this just made things worse because crying contracted my throat around the napkin. When he finally pulled the napkin out of my mouth, it was soaked with blood.

It would take a long time before I could overcome any of these fears. I had to ease forward in steps. With the napkin, the first step was just to leave it there on the table while I ate. The next step was to touch it. Finally, after a few more times, I was able to put the napkin on my lap. The same with the motorcycle helmet. First, I had to teach myself to look at one without getting a panic attack. My method was to make sure any helmet was not within reach, was just something I could see. Slowly and gradually I was able to look at helmets, then, after a while, to touch one, and eventually to wear one and ride a motorcycle—a great thrill for me. In time I got used to some of the food smells as well. Overcoming these phobias was for me a victory over my torturer. I could say to myself that he had not won after all; he had not broken me. He had lost. I had won. The fear he had used as a weapon would never, ever control me.

THAT FIRST CHRISTMAS as a free woman I bought a white Christmas tree and lots of lights and lit up my apartment like crazy. It was a quiet holiday, and of course my heart was with Joey, wherever he was. But I was glad to count my blessings. I was free, I was whole, I was putting my life back together.

Early in the new year I even took my first trip to New York City, with my lawyer, to meet with "my" publisher. It was my first-ever ride on an airplane too, and before I ever got on the plane I had a mildly disastrous but mostly kind of funny experience—namely, a brush with the security folks at the airport in Cleveland. The trip was to last a few days, and I had packed enough to stay for a month. But I somehow managed to lift my carry-on up onto the conveyor belt, and off it went on its way through the X-ray machine. There was an awful grumbling sound from the machine, and one of the TSA agents asked me to "please step aside, ma'am."

"You have liquids in your suitcase," she announced to me. I sure did. I had a bottle of water and a bottle of mouth-wash packed away, plus a tube of toothpaste. All of them were prohibited items to bring on a plane, not because of what they were but because the containers were bigger than 3.4 ounces. I had had absolutely no idea. The agent gave me a choice: "You'll either have to check the suitcase, or I will need to confiscate these items and throw them out."

Go back and check the bag? Throw the stuff out? I couldn't believe it. What for? "I didn't know I couldn't have liquids," I protested to the agent.

For a minute she didn't say anything, just stared at me. Then, in a tone that sounded like she either didn't believe me or thought I was conning her, she said, "Ma'am, this has been the rule for the last ten years at least!"

That's when my lawyer took over. "You have no idea," she said to the TSA agent, "where this woman has been for the last ten years."

She and I both cracked up, and then my lawyer explained it all to the agent. Of course, she knew about me and Gina and Amanda and the whole story. She seemed embarrassed, but she managed to chuckle. "I apologize for scaring the crap out of you," she said.

"That's okay," I told her. "Crap happens."

I handed over the prohibited items, and we took off. I figured New York would have everything I needed, and of course it did. It was amazing to be there. In a plush office in a real publishing firm, I met with my agent and the team who would be helping me produce a book. I saw the sights, and I even saw my first Broadway show—*Kinky Boots*—and got to go backstage afterward to meet the cast. Talk about amazing!

Not long after I got back to Cleveland I got a call from a friend inviting me to a birthday party downtown, not far from the apartment complex where I lived. I had met this friend, Gina Baker, when I was at the hospice and had first started going out to clubs with Anita and Erna. So she was part of a little group I had always felt very comfortable with and liked very much, and I figured that because it was probably time I reconnected with other people, this was the crowd to do it with. I said yes. It was my first real "night out" since moving into the apartment, and I ended up having a great time. Having gone straight from high school to motherhood to captivity, I had never really known how good it can be to party and have fun, so it was a kind of discovery for me, one I liked very much.

From that moment on, there was no stopping me. I enjoyed meeting new people, although of course it was more that *they* were new to *me*. I wasn't new to *them* because they had all seen the Dr. Phil interviews, seen the headlines and follow-up stories, and were familiar with lots of details about my captivity and rescue. But it felt good to show up at some noisy club, get together with people who were becoming regular acquaintances, and meet new people night after night. I guess this is what people do in their late teens and twenties— all the nightly or weekend partying that I had missed. And I guess now I was making up for it. You could say I squeezed my twenties into the first year after my rescue. I may have squeezed in too much at times, but it was a valuable learning experience.

Just about my favorite place was the Corner Alley, not far from my apartment complex. It's a bowling alley/sports bar/restaurant/game room all rolled into one, and it is really a fun place to go. For me, what made it even better was that the staff there got to know me and grew pretty protective of me. One of the employees walked me home one night when there was a kind of noisy crowd outside, and some of the folks who worked there would check the streets outside before I headed home. It was frustrating to think that kind of protectiveness was necessary, but it felt good to know it was there.

One night, after a few rounds of bowling, I wandered into the House of Blues, the karaoke spot near where I lived. I had passed it a million times, but tonight, when everything downtown seemed to be crazy busy, I could hear people belting it out inside and thought I'd like to listen more closely, so I pulled open the doors and walked in. It turned out to be one of the best moves of my life because it brought me into contact with two of my closest and dearest friends.

When I walked in I saw a man who looked to be in his fifties coming toward me. I always got nervous when people approached me; I always wondered what they might ask me and what their manner would be.

"I'm Jim," he said. "What are you going to sing tonight?"

There is only one word for the way Jim looks at you: kind. "Oh," I said, "I don't know. I'm not even sure I feel like singing right now."

"But I just know you have a pretty voice," Jim said. "Go on up there and sing. No need to be afraid of anybody here. We all love you."

I muttered that I was having vision problems. "I'm not sure I'd even be able to see the words."

He nodded, then he grinned. "There's a song I like that I bet you would know. Will you sing it with me?" The song was "Summer Nights" from *Grease,* and we sang it together—my karaoke debut. I don't think Olivia and John need to worry about the competition, but it was uplifting to stand there and sing the song with that wonderful man. I sang most of it from memory because I couldn't entirely see or hear the words.

When the song ended, someone in the audience shouted out to me: "Sing 'Roar'! Can you sing 'Roar' for me? It would be so powerful to hear you sing that song." I barely knew the song, but the woman in the audience was shrieking, "She's gonna sing my song, she's gonna sing my song!" Kenny, the DJ at House of Blues, had caught on to my problem and had figured out what I needed in order to follow along, so he played the song softly enough that I could feel the vibrations and hear some of the words. And then, as I sang it, I realized that it was a powerful song for me. It told my story. Held down, I had gotten up. I was a fighter, and I am a champion, and as I stood there singing, I felt that I really did have the eye of the tiger and that I was roaring like a lion. I think everybody who heard me sing that song that night felt so too.

I still sing "Roar" at karaoke nights with friends. Whenever I do, Jim cries, but he assures me they're tears of joy.

After the singing Jim and I sat and talked. And talked and talked. For hours. It felt like I had always known him, but I almost couldn't trust that feeling because—well, first because he was a man—still hard for me to feel calm about—and because of my ongoing fear that, like a lot of people, he might want something from me. I never really had a father, but as Jim and I kept talking, that was the word that kept coming into my mind. It came into my mind even more strongly when he walked me home because he said it was too late for me to walk by myself. When we got to my building he asked, "Are you going to come to karaoke next week?"

"Why not?" I said. And I did. Jim and Kenny and I grew our friendship over those next weeks and months. Around this time I was really behaving like a party animal, and both of them kept an eye on me and looked out for my well-being. Jim always made sure I got home safely and took extra care when I had had one drink too many—easy to do when you're my size—and both showed me that there are men in this world who do not misuse women or dishonor trust.

Years later Jim would write about how, when he first saw me, he "felt an immediate need to protect her, like an older brother or a dad." He wrote that although I seemed "outgoing and vibrant, ready to take on the world," he sensed that "inside, it was the total opposite. She still lived in fear, very hesitant to trust, especially men." Clearly Jim could see inside my soul back then. He still can.

Together we sometimes sing the song that has meant more to me than any other, "My Heart Will Go On" by Celine Dion. It is the song that saved my life when I was in

Castro's house. I had reached perhaps the lowest point in eleven years of misery. I just didn't want to live anymore. I was wondering how I could find a way to kill myself when, suddenly, the song came on the radio. I listened to the lyrics, and I wondered, *What would Joey think if he learned his mother killed herself? Could his heart go on if he knew his mother had taken her life? If he believed his mother had not seen him as a reason to stay alive?* That thought—that song—stopped me. It represented my son to me. It represented my love for him. This is what I had told Dr. Phil in our interview, and it is what I told Celine Dion in person when we met.

When I first described my history with that song to Jim, he urged me to sing it. He spoke as if I had to sing it—for my own sake, and for my son's. So I did. Kenny again did the music, low, so only I could hear it. You can't sing if you're crying, so I kept the sobs out of my voice, but the tears rolled down my face anyway as I sang. The tears were for Joey, whom I missed so much, and they were tears of relief that I had not given in to the darkness on those days when I wanted to die. I was alive, and I had friends—these two wonderful men backing me up as I sang this song as if my life depended on it, as it once had. I had a lot to be thankful for.

NOT ALL the people I met in those partying days were as wonderful. Not even close. In fact, as the weeks and months wore on, I realized a couple of important things. One was that I was drinking too much with my new friends—drinking too much without them as well. The other was that a lot of my new friends were friends to my face but not behind my back.

I finally began to realize that I went out with a lot of these people just because they asked me. Someone would call, I would be feeling lonely with nothing to do, and I'd just go and meet up with them instead of staying home alone. They would all want me to tell "my story," but if I thought that confiding in people would mean they would be understanding and would have my back, I was dead wrong. What a lot of them wanted was to show off—"Look who I'm with. I'm with Michelle Knight." And then behind my back they'd be calling me stupid because, as one said, I "let this happen" to me. I realized they were there not for friendship but for what they could get out of being with me. New friends, I was learning, could be as disappointing as old friends had turned out to be.

I guess I first noticed it one night at House of Blues when I was there with a good-sized bunch of "friends," all gathered around a table. One by one, each of them went outside for a cigarette, or so they said. I was cool with that; most of these new friends smoked, so they would often go outside, then come back in. But this time everyone was gone for longer than it takes to smoke a cigarette. Fifteen minutes. Twenty minutes. Thirty.

So I walked out there, and they were gone. I went back in and paid what I owed. The management at the House of

Blues knew me well by this time, and I told them, "You know me. I always pay my way, but I don't pay for anybody else's bill. When you see those people next time, make them pay what they owe." Management agreed.

There it was again—that *thing* that says if you're "famous," you're a target. I was famous for having been tortured and abused for eleven years, and now people were trying to do it again. That's how I saw it. They were trying to take advantage of me, and they thought they could. It made me angry, and it made me feel unsafe. I was getting tired of people coming into my life with what I thought of as a fake mask that covered who they truly were and thinking it was okay to take advantage of me and hurt me. It wasn't. But I had to let go—to forgive others for their cruelty and forgive myself for bad judgment. I couldn't let it consume me.

One day, not long afterward, I was walking to my favorite cupcake store to get a treat. I had just crossed the street when I heard that awful sound of lots of cars honking at once. I turned and saw a young woman crossing the street behind me but against the light. She wore baggy pants and a baggy sweatshirt with a big scarf around her neck, and she had tripped and fallen, which is why the cars had stopped and were honking.

I ran over to her to see if she was okay. She was, so she brushed herself off, and we crossed the street together. She was talking a mile a minute, explaining how she had been trying to reach me so she could talk to me, and we walked together into the cupcake store.

"Oh, Michelle Knight, Michelle Knight," she was saying. "You are my hero. I just had to meet you! Where do you live?" she asked.

"Not far," I said, leaving it vague. We ordered cupcakes and talked for a little—well, she talked—as we ate. She said she had just moved to the area and wondered what there was to do. I told her about the Corner Alley and a few other local spots.

And after a bit I gathered my things, told her I had to go, and wished her well.

"Can I come with you?" she asked.

Something now didn't seem right. "I have an appointment," I told her, "so that won't be possible."

"How about a photo of us together?"

I was used to this, so I said, "Sure," and she snapped a selfie before I hurried out of the shop. I looked back once I had crossed the street, and there she was, standing in the window of the cupcake shop staring at me. The truth is that I was on my way home, but I darted in and out of different buildings to throw her off in case she was following me.

A few days later, early in the morning, I headed out of my building. My book, *Finding Me,* had just been published, and I was on my way to an interview. I had on a really nice dress and was wearing high heels. I felt good. It was rush hour, and the streets were filled with people on their way to work. Even in the bustle I could tell that people were stopping to stare at me. I was kind of accustomed to this, but it still made me nervous. Everyone else in the street was allowed to be anonymous—why couldn't I be too? I had stepped up my pace in a useless attempt to escape the stares *and* to make it to my interview on time when one heel got caught in a hole in the sidewalk, and the next thing I knew, I was flat on the ground.

People stopped. Many started taking pictures. One pointed and laughed. "She's drunk!" he said gleefully. I pegged him for an overgrown playground bully.

What is wrong with some people? I thought to myself. Do they want me to fall and be humiliated so they can post the pictures? Why? Will it make them feel better about themselves?

My immediate problem, however, was how to get up—if possible, gracefully. Then someone reached out a hand to me. Gratefully, I took it, stood up, and looked into the face of the woman from the cupcake shop. My heart started racing.

"Michelle Knight, it is so good to see you!" she said. "I have been looking for you!"

"I am late," I told her. "Thanks for your help. I have to go." I made a mad dash through the morning commuters to escape.

Up to now I had felt pretty safe in my apartment building. But a few nights later I came home to learn that a woman had come into the lobby, managing to enter without a key while another tenant was exiting. The woman had then walked through the building, asking tenants which apartment was mine. The manager on duty told her that I wasn't in, but the woman showed the manager my book and said, "I need Michelle Knight to sign my book right now!" He repeated that

I was not in and asked her if she wanted to sign in or leave a note. Angrily, she said no and left. Before he even showed me the surveillance tape, I knew who it was. That's right. Cupcake shop lady.

The next time I went bowling at the Corner Alley I was told a woman had been there asking for me. One of the staff walked me home that night. Having someone by my side to look out for me was not something I wanted, but that evening it was something I needed.

From then on, I went outside only if somebody walked with me. Jim, Kenny, and the Corner Alley employees took turns at this. Pretty much whenever I had to go out in public I would alert one of them, who would then watch the crowd and sometimes even move people away from me. I hated it. I'd been vulnerable all my life. I know that stalkers should be pitied, not despised; I understand they feel a terrible loneliness and rejection. But I was tired of suffering and feeling afraid. All I wanted now was to feel free, yet even in my apartment building I was beginning to act like a caged animal.

That was about to change—big time. *Finding Me* was published on May 6, 2014, one year to the day after I was rescued. I had spent all my life within a few square miles of Cleveland, Ohio, and I had spent much of my life silenced, both physically and emotionally. But now I was about to embark on a book tour. I was off to see the world, yes, and I was also preparing to speak out about my life—over and over and over again to tell my story of what had happened to me to the millions of people who wanted to hear it.

CHAPTER FIVE

Healing After Trauma

I learned to love myself in order to love others . . .

SOMETIME AROUND THE holiday season last year somebody—maybe Jim or Anita or Erna, although I don't exactly remember which of them—said to me that I seemed so much stronger, physically and mentally, than they had ever seen me. Any one of those three would certainly know, because they had seen me when I was pretty much at my worst. When I met them I was in or just out of hospice care in Hinckley, was often back and forth to the hospital, and was still physically sick and fairly weak. I was mentally pretty broken as well.

But nearly four years later, when I heard those words—"physically and mentally stronger"—it struck me right away that they were true. I had come a long way since my rescue and had done a lot of healing since I was in hospice. What's more, I continued to feel like I was getting physically and mentally stronger every day. This tells me that the process of healing after trauma keeps going. My process of healing from my trauma could well go on for the rest of my life. That's fine with me.

Yet at the time I was kidnapped I don't think I would have known what either of those words—trauma or healing—really meant. Five years after my rescue I have learned the meaning of both words firsthand—up close and very, very personal.

Any physical injury that sends you to a hospital can be a trauma.

I had had plenty of those. I was close to death the day we were rescued. I climbed into that ambulance and was then in and out of hospitals for weeks. Doctors and nurses and "procedures" defined the first days of my freedom. Stitches, needles, tubes going into me, tubes going out of me—I had wounds inside and out. There wasn't much of my body that didn't require medical attention.

But there's another kind of trauma too: the injury to the mind. It's the injury that occurs when you've been through something so awful that you can't really cope with it. The stress is too big to manage. You can't keep up with what it's doing to you. The horror of it takes over, and you just don't have the emotional strength to sort it out.

All sorts of experiences can do this to people: sexual and physical abuse as a child, bullying, verbal abuse, having an alcoholic parent, kidnapping, violence. I actually experienced everything on that list, and I had tried to escape all of it all my life. I had reported abuse to the authorities, I had run away from home to live on the streets, and I had refused to break—even when Castro thought he had taken all my strength. But the experience of all those horrors had marked me. It had left its imprint on my body, on my mind, on my soul. And that imprint was affecting how I was managing to survive even after the experience had ended.

There was one thing I knew for certain: I could not undo the things that had happened to me. They could not unhappen. But I also knew I needed to find a way to live with that fact and move forward. In a word, I needed help.

Of course, I tried talk therapy. Twice. I was on my own in the apartment by then, trying to piece together a life I could go forward with, and the first therapist I saw gave me the impression that I wasn't down or depressed *enough*. I remember one day telling her that I was actually feeling kind of upbeat about myself and my future. "Really?" she said. "That tells me that you may not be working hard enough at understanding what has gone wrong with your life." I began to feel that it wasn't worth her time to consult with me if I wasn't completely destroyed.

That was not a good fit.

The next therapist I tried was male, and that was probably not a good idea for me. I hadn't yet even talked to my male friends about what had happened to me, so opening up to this man was not going to happen. Also, he liked to place blame, and he particularly liked to place blame for everything that had happened to me *on me*. I was to blame for not getting away from my family. I was to blame for letting myself lose custody of my child. When I thought he was about to tell me that I was to blame for getting kidnapped, I decided I did not need to hear that and I quit. Cold turkey.

So for the moment, anyway, I gave up therapy.

I should say, rather, that I gave up talking to *therapists*, because the truth is I was doing my own form of therapy every time I told my story to anyone, and on the book tour that is exactly what I did—over and over and over again. I spent practically the entire month of May giving interviews, often several a day, starting with a *Today* show interview with Savannah Guthrie on May 5, which was actually the day before the book was officially released. To say I was nervous does not even come close to describing how I was feeling. I was sweating, on edge, trying like hell to picture everybody around me as a minion in *Despicable Me* or a Hostess Twinkie in overalls—my own method for reducing what overwhelms me to manageable proportions—and I was so terrified that I kept running to the ladies' room. But Savannah talked to me one on one before the interview got going, so I got an inkling of the kind of down-to-earth person she was, and once the interview began, it was okay.

There were thirty-three more interviews for television, radio, and print as the tour went on, and I cannot even count the number of questions I answered before we ended with a Paris television interview on May 26, the end of the tour—well, of *that* part of the tour anyway.

It was the first time I had ever been out of the United States, and my first foreign stop was Toronto, Canada, which did not seem all that foreign. London, which came next, did seem foreign, and I hope my British readers will not be offended if I say I had more trouble understanding what people said to me there than I did in Germany or France. In both the latter countries a translator accompanied me, but I really needed one in London because I found the accent hard to follow, especially because everybody talked so quickly that I just couldn't keep up. But it was exciting to be in London and to feel surrounded by history.

Germany came next: two stops, Munich and Cologne. I seemed to be allergic to much of the food, but I loved just about everything I ate and couldn't stop munching. The centerpiece of my visit there was a televised interview with the families of several missing children. The people were all very loving and supportive of their children, but one of the stories told that night was so like my own that it simply blanked my brain. I had to get up and walk out for a few moments.

Then we went to Paris, with all those glorious monuments and everybody speaking that beautiful language. I was excited to see so much art all over the place, and I found the sound of the language *ooh-la-la.*

Even returning to the States wasn't the end of the tour. After a little time at home in Cleveland, I was back on the road in August and September, when I traveled to Puerto Rico, and in October I had my first "professional" speaking engagement—not an interview but me making a speech about the subject I unfortunately am an expert on: abuse.

I also "talked" in other ways, the same ways I had always done when I needed a refuge and some solace as a child—by writing and drawing, through poetry and art. All these retellings of my story, both to myself and to anonymous audiences around the world, helped lift a lot of pain off my shoulders.

But I understood that although finding the words to describe what had happened was important and that each retelling seemed to lighten the pain a bit more, I still wasn't healed. I had reclaimed my life, but I still hadn't totally put the past in its place so I could live in the present.

What's more, the tour was also super-exhausting. There were days when I did as many as half a dozen interviews—

by phone or in person—one after the other after the other. I never wanted to cancel even a single interview because I was always sure there was someone out there listening who might need the help I could maybe give. But it was an awfully tiring schedule.

Some of the interviews were tougher than others. And one interview, in which a male interviewer on some radio show asked me what it had been like to be raped all those years in Castro's house, made me absolutely furious. It was just too stupid a question for anyone to ask; coming from a man, it really offended me. "How can you even say such a thing?" I roared back at him. "How can you ask someone who lived through it to answer that? That is such an inappropriate question—I won't answer it!"

That was the worst, the absolute bottom of the whole month and more of book selling. But it was all pretty draining. I was drinking too much, eating too much junk food, sleeping badly, if at all, feeling lonely in the middle of crowds, and in general going down an unhealthy and unhappy path. I knew it too—I couldn't not know it. One day I just lifted a prayer to God, telling Him that I felt I was losing my way and asking for a sign that would show me I was on the wrong path. The next day I went off to do another interview, and a woman in the audience got up and told her story and described the exact feelings I was feeling. I took that as the sign I had asked for, so now I needed a way to find the right path.

I confided all this to my lawyer and told her that I felt I had to do something—make some sort of change—because

I felt like I was losing myself on this wrong path. Somehow I think she got word to Dr. Phil. He had told me I could call him anytime, and he didn't just say that as a throwaway line for a onetime guest on his show. He meant it. I know because we talked frequently about my "process" of healing, on both up days and down days. This is a guy I felt really cared about my life. I *knew* he cared because he had shown that he did— in words and in actions.

This is also a guy plugged into and affiliated with lots of "treatment resources," as he calls them. One is Onsite, which runs therapeutic workshops, including for people who have experienced trauma. Dr. Phil recommended that I go to their center outside of Nashville, Tennessee, to spend time in their Healing Trauma program—and, in particular, because of my love of animals, to try the Equine Therapy program there as well. In fact, he and my lawyer made all the arrangements for me to do that.

I got on the plane to fly down to Nashville. I had a window seat, and next to me was a very sweet-looking old lady. We said hello to one another, and she told me that she recognized me from all the news stories. The plane took off and rose up and up through the clouds until we couldn't see the ground anymore, just the blue sky above. I turned to the old lady and said to her, just out of the blue, "I'm closer to heaven now." Just as suddenly she began to cry. "They are tears of joy," she assured me, "because I'm so glad to be sitting next to an angel." To be able to do such a small thing and cause such a big impact seemed to me a good omen for what was ahead.

An Onsite representative met me on arrival in Nashville and took me to the amazingly beautiful "campus" of the center. It was enormous. Massive. Acres and acres of green grass and clumps of high trees stretched across rolling hills. There was a huge, handsome two-story main building with a wraparound porch, red shutters, and a fenced platform on the top part of the roof. It all looked to me very much the way I thought buildings in the South would look. And there were several outbuildings, including a reddish-brown barn. I figured that whatever happened, this was a perfect place to spend time.

I was there for a month, and the days were full. Mornings began with yoga, deep breathing, aromatherapy, meditation, movement, acupuncture, art therapy—all kinds of different healing exercises and activities. There were games or activities that got my group—about fifteen of us in all—to trust one another and games that helped us build teamwork. And there were sessions for dealing with the effects of trauma in which, one after another, people told their stories.

As you know, I wasn't all that keen on that sort of thing. I didn't feel comfortable talking in front of a group of people. Yes, I had told my story a lot when I was on the book tour. But that was different. First, I was talking about the book; it had detailed the eleven years in Castro's house, and I just answered questions about the events of those years over and over. And I was talking to an *audience*—mostly an unseen audience of nameless people. Here at Onsite we were all together in the same room, all right there, side by side, all harmed by past trauma. It was much more intimate and somehow it just felt different. "I don't even talk about this stuff with my brother," I told them. "Why would I talk about my issues right now?"

"Okay," the leader said, "if you don't want to talk about your issues, why don't you tell us how you feel?"

"I feel crummy," I said. "I feel like I'm being pushed to talk about my personal life in front of a bunch of strangers, and I don't care for it."

"Good process," the leader said. I guess they were processing the information I had just given; I didn't feel I was processing anything.

MEANWHILE I went to the first session of equine therapy.

I had absolutely no idea what to expect. There were about ten of us signed up for equine therapy, and we all hiked over to the horse barn. When I say "hiked," I mean *hiked*. The campus was so big, so spread out, that it took a while to get there. But it was a lovely day. The trees were changing color, the sun was bright, and the air was cool. Sweater weather, where all I needed was a light cardigan to feel comfortable.

When we got to the barn the wranglers led all the horses outside into the fenced-in paddock where we were waiting.

The horses started munching hay and grass, and then the facilitator, the person in charge of equine therapy, told us all to start interacting with the horses.

I had never ridden a horse in my life. I'm not sure I had ever been this close to horses before. But I love all animals, so I started petting the horses one at a time. They seemed nice and passive, a little less frightening close up than from a distance. "Okay," said the facilitator, "now choose one of the horses to be 'your horse' for the rest of your time here." Everybody started choosing their horse, based on color, I think, and I had my eye on a nice brown horse that was also fairly small. One thing I was sure of was that I didn't want a huge horse.

But in the end "my" horse chose me, not the other way around. He was named Waylon, and he came up behind me and lowered his head to graze my face with his. I thought that was pretty cute, but I confess that I was a little scared of just how big he was—especially compared to four-foot-seven me. There was nothing I could do about it, though. Not only had he picked me, but he was also the last horse standing—and the biggest and tallest. Every other horse was now taken.

He certainly was a beautiful animal. Everything about him was golden—his creamy gold coat, a golden-brown mane and tail that flew in the wind, and beautiful golden-brown eyes. I was definitely scared at first that he would stomp on me. Given where both of us started, it wouldn't have taken much. Of course, no such thing ever happened. Something quite the opposite happened.

I have always loved animals because they don't judge you. They don't criticize, and they certainly don't abuse. I've said it before: the only animals that cause hurt for the fun of it are humans—no animal ever would. But still, when I first met Waylon I felt he was acting kind of distant from me. He had touched my face with his, but as we started working together, he seemed somehow standoffish. We were not communicating at all—until I finally realized that he was distant because I was distant.

The horse had it right: I *was* distant. I *wanted* to be distant—from everyone. I wanted to keep my story to myself. It had been enough to write the book to an audience of people I couldn't see and would never meet. I didn't want to deal with this anymore; I just wanted to move on.

Understand that I never rode this horse. I never got on his back at all the whole time I was there. That wasn't what this therapy process was all about. The horse and I were one on one, on our own two feet in my case, four feet in his case, the whole time. I fed him, groomed him—I loved to brush his mane and tail—and mucked out his stall. I took care of him, earning his trust, and I cared for him, which gave me a great sense of accomplishment too. In return, he taught me patience, and he taught me to trust myself.

The therapy that being with horses provides—and the reason recovery programs like Onsite use horses—is based on a horse's ability to mirror exactly what people are feeling at any given moment. They're fantastic mimics. You know how good they are at mirroring what other horses are feeling. If you've ever seen a movie or a nature program about horses, you've seen how a herd of horses operates: no matter how many horses are part of the herd, they move totally in sync with one another. It's because they're prey animals, not predators, so they are all about staying safe, and staying safe means they need to be constantly alert to danger. Once one horse in the herd senses danger and starts acting nervous or antsy, every other horse in the herd mirrors that, and the feeling gets broadcast through the herd. The other horses will become agitated too, and they will run like crazy to get away from the danger, sticking together the whole time. It almost looks like it's just a single animal running. So being able to sense what other horses are feeling is a plus; it's an evolutionary advantage that reduces the danger that a horse would face on its own. That's why they're so good at it, so attuned to what's happening around them. And it's why it's part of their DNA.

The amazing part is that where humans are concerned, it's the same. Horses can catch what a human is feeling the same as they catch what their brother horses are feeling. Once a horse assesses a human as safe, it will accept the human as part of the herd. That's what Waylon had done when he walked over to me, when he "chose" me. He drew me into his safe circle, and that was it: I was now in his herd.

People who have suffered trauma are alert to danger in the same way horses are—all the time. We can't help it—it's in our bodies. Things that are everyday sights and sounds to most people can be triggers for us, and when one of those triggers gets pulled, we don't just remember what happened to us; our bodies experience what happened to us all over again, and we react to defend ourselves. I've mentioned that motorcycle helmets and cloth napkins and certain foods and smells were triggers for me; they could put me back in Castro's house in a second and send me into a tailspin of fear and anxiety. When I first got to the hospice in Hinckley there was a Porta Potty in my room for emergency use, but I told Rachel and her husband that they had to get it away from me. It's what Castro had given me to use when he let me "graduate" from using just a plastic bucket. There was also a rocking chair in the hospice. I realize now that's a pretty standard item in a rest home for frail elderly people, but Castro had a rocking chair that he used for sexual abuse, and I made Rachel and her husband get the one in the hospice out of my sight. It isn't logical, but it's automatic. And that's what my therapy with Waylon was going to try to ease.

Waylon could sense in an instant if I was anxious, as I was in that first moment when we met. I was downright scared of how big and strong he was. But he had walked over to me, accepting me as a member of his herd. When I looked into his golden-brown eyes and felt I was looking into the soul of a creature that only wished me well, I was ready to trust the program we were about to go through together.

The therapy part of the mirroring worked like this: in the various therapy exercises we were going to do, I could look at Waylon to see how I was feeling, and if I could change the emotion I was feeling, it would show up in him—in the way he was feeling. So looking at him and seeing his feelings was both an incentive for me and a guide for changing how I responded to the world.

For me personally, this was a really smart way to do the kind of therapy I needed. I've told you how, when I was growing up, I was always ordered to keep my mouth shut. I was told that "children should be seen and not heard," and that phrase went through my head every time I tried to talk about something or express how I felt as a kid. I always worried that if I didn't say a thing exactly the way people wanted me to say it—if what I said didn't please people—that I was wrong or that I shouldn't be saying it. Or, at best, that it just wouldn't make sense, and no one would get it, and people would just see me a certain way no matter what I said and would try to tell me who I am. So it was as if talking—trying to tell others how I felt—actually took away my ability to make my own choices.

But with Waylon and the equine healing therapy, there was no need ever to try to express my feelings in words. What I was feeling just showed up in my body, for the horse to pick up on. This was the tool the facilitators relied on as they asked us to do various activities.

The activities were about helping us learn to trust or calming our fears of being hurt. They were about learning to love ourselves or having confidence in ourselves. In each of the activities assigned, Waylon would sense the effect every situation or every memory had on me and would react.

There was no way to hide my emotions from him—he was my mirror. Whatever I could not control or manage or regulate in me would show up in him. I could only help him settle down if I took charge of my own emotions. In this way I would learn not just to manage my emotions but actually to change them.

The way it worked at Onsite was that there was a kind of track where you would walk your horse. There was a little bridge that took up the middle between the two halves of the track. One half, on the left, was safe space; the other half, on the right, was unsafe space. So when the facilitator gave you an activity to do—like telling the horse the story of your abuse—the horse shows what the telling does to you. If you're shaky or afraid to tell the truth, the horse goes over to the unsafe space, and it probably means you're not ready yet to tell the whole truth of what happened to you. But you're going to need to tell the whole truth if you want your horse to settle and lead you to safety.

For me, it started with activities to try to build my confidence and to learn to love myself. I held onto a rope attached to Waylon's halter, and the facilitator asked me some questions, and we started walking. I gave an answer that was in some way defective or unsound or incomplete—either I wasn't telling the truth or I was disoriented when I said what I said or I was afraid when I was answering—and Waylon caught that at once and led us to the unsafe side. Then when I "corrected" my answer—paid attention and told the whole truth—he led me back to the safe side. As you can imagine, after a while you feel how important it is to dig down for the truth and get to the safe side.

There was one activity in which I had to get Waylon to come toward me but stop at my command. The idea of this was for me to experience saying no. It was to remind myself that I had the right and the power to set boundaries that others would need to respect. I could do that with Waylon because I knew he was not judging me. He couldn't say anything bad or ugly to me, couldn't and wouldn't make me feel afraid or ashamed of what had happened to me in my life. I commanded him to stop, and he walked us right over to the safe side, then stopped, assuring me that the boundaries I had set were sound and strong.

Of course, one of the hardest activities is to tell your horse your own trauma story and let him lead you to safety. If he senses that your story isn't truthful, that you are afraid to tell it, or that you're not really answering, he will lead you to the unsafe side—until you change.

When I got that "assignment," Waylon and I started walking, and I told him how I had felt as a child. I told him I had been abused. I told him about the many really bad things that had happened to me as a child, that multiple family members had hurt me. And as we kept on walking, the horse stopped, turned to me, paused, and it was like he was saying to me, *You've got something else to say. Let's get it said so we can go over the bridge.* He meant so we could cross to the safe side.

And all I can tell you is that something came over me to tell him everything. It just poured out of me. My whole

life. The abuse I suffered as a kid. My son Joey. The kidnap.
The house. Gina and Amanda. Everything I wrote about in
Finding Me and everything you're reading about in this book
about what had happened since I got out of Castro's house
as well. All the confusion. All the pain. All the anger. My lifetime of being messed up, of not knowing who I was or where
I was going.

This wasn't like writing a book or answering questions on
television. This was talking to a being who got it and didn't
judge me. Not a being who was going to ask me why I didn't
find a way to get out of Castro's house or would tell me that
he or she would have done more. No questions were asked.
Waylon was willing to listen; he knew how to listen. It was like
telling my story *through* the horse. "All I know now," I said to
Waylon, "is that *I* define who I am." And we walked across
that bridge to the safe space, and it was done.

I can't explain why it had come over me to tell this horse
what I never directly told a human in my life—except that
I knew he wasn't going to tell anybody or hurt anybody or
use me or anything that I said. And when he led me across
the bridge to the safe space, I felt a whole new sense of who
I am. My fears seemed to evaporate. I felt strong. I felt like
Waylon had helped me catch all the pieces of me that were
falling apart and that he and I in combination were putting
the pieces back together.

The therapy with Waylon also made it possible for me
to talk to the other trauma survivors who got together each

morning. The more I listened to the others talk—the group included both men and women—it was clear they were all coming out of terrible situations. Physical abuse, sexual abuse, mental abuse, violence, crime—they had suffered many different kinds of pain that they were trying to let go of. Also, they knew who I was—they had read the stories or seen the headlines or watched the television reports. They understood who I was and accepted me for who I was, so they didn't push me to talk. They just waited until I was ready, and finally I was.

I spoke up and said I wanted to share something. They all looked at me. "The first thing I want to say is that I had to learn to love myself so I can love others, so I can eventually have positive friends instead of negative friends." And when I said that, everybody applauded, which was really good. It gave me encouraging feedback. "This is the first time," I told them, "that I'm sharing my story with a group of people who are right here in the room with me, and it is because you are basically going through the same kind of thing I'm going through. And having people that know what you went through, people you know are on your side, people who are loving and compassionate, makes me believe I can do this. I can talk about my past and share my trauma with you."

And I could, even though there were men there, which made it difficult, and even a person who had caused abuse, and at first it was very, very difficult for me to be in the same room with him. But I was beginning to understand that even people who are doing the abuse need help too.

Most definitely it had taken me a while to feel that I knew these people. For me it always takes time to get to know somebody, but as I listened, I understood that they were not there for what they could get from me. I understood that, unlike the therapists I had tried to talk to, all these folks had experienced some sort of trauma—and they too had not been able to cope. They knew what it felt like to have your life yanked out from under you. Like me, they were survivors, which meant they weren't going to judge me. That said to me that they would understand what I was saying. I would be safe talking to them. Also, the rule there was: what happens here stays here. Once I grew confident about that, it was the last bit of safety I needed, and I opened up totally. It felt like the right thing to do, and it felt good.

I DID THERAPY with Waylon each week while I was at Onsite. Each session with him was highly emotional. Also pretty tiring. But I grew stronger each time.

One of the last times I saw him we did another activity that was very important to me. No rope connecting us this time, just a very light, narrow string of yarn. I was in the middle of telling Waylon how I wanted to help others who have been abused, especially children, and to give them a safe space too. Waylon suddenly bent his long, beautiful neck down to grab a snack and munch some hay, and the little string between us broke. Without stopping or interrupting what I was saying, I picked the broken string up off the ground and retied it, and we just kept going—Waylon still keeping us in our safe space. The moment seemed meaningful, as if to say there is always the choice to keep going, no matter what happens in your life, and there is always a way to reconnect. All the negativity in the world, all the abuse people put upon you can't stop you. Every day is a new day when you can go forward. You can always fix a broken string.

For our final visit I was assigned to create a picture in my mind of someone who had hurt me and then try to transmit that picture to Waylon. Then I was to tell that person that I no longer feared him or her, that I couldn't be hurt by the person anymore. In my case, there wasn't just one person who had hurt me, so the portrait I made in my head was a multiple. It contained the various members of my family who I felt had hurt me.

I lined up the picture in my mind and waited for Waylon's response, and when it came I felt I now had the power to knock all these people out of my life, to say no and to stand up to each one of them. I felt this as a sort of burst of strength—not the kind you feel when you flex a muscle but rather strength within me. I felt it was there to use any day I needed it. Strength that would let me control whether I will enter safe or unsafe space. Strength that would let me slow down and take time to be in my own head so I can find the power to overcome and rise above. That's the kind of strength I felt flowing into me. If I had not felt my own power to control who I let into my life, Waylon wouldn't have let me cross to the safe space. Even today, whenever I feel my strength sagging just a little bit, I think of Waylon, the horse who wouldn't let me give in or give up.

The timing of that particular exercise was just right, because during the month I was down in Tennessee a whole bunch of "family members" came out of the woodwork. The publication of *Finding Me* had set in motion a whole new flurry of people showing up on television to claim they were my relatives. I had never met any of them, didn't know their names, and could only guess what they were after in claiming that we were related. The guess was that, whoever they were, they were interested in money in some way—that's usually what people are after.

I have no problem or embarrassment or hesitation in saying that a horse showed me things about myself that I needed to learn. When I arrived at the trauma center I wasn't even close to loving myself. I felt my life was ending, and I thought nobody would care. All of that changed through my relationship with Waylon. I bonded with that horse in a unique friendship. Emotionally, I felt totally safe with him. At that time, in fact, I felt he was the only friend I had on earth. Yet what he gave me has made it possible for me to find other true friends—my safe circle—and, I believe, to build my relationship with my husband.

Waylon never pushed me into a corner where I didn't want to be, and when I left him I made him a promise. I told him that I knew I was still hurting and that I still felt negativity from a lot of people, but I looked in his eyes and said,

"I don't want that in my heart. I'm letting it go." I promised him I would choose positive ways to overcome things and to reach my goals. I promised to make positive choices, and I admitted that, even since my rescue, I had made some bad decisions, some dumb decisions. "I'm going to choose differently," I said. "That's a promise." Then Waylon bent his beautiful head down to rest on my shoulder, and again he brushed my face with his. And it was like he was telling me that he understood. He knew I would be okay because he knew I was strong.

My month at the trauma center had been super-exhausting in so many ways, but when it was over I truly felt ready to move on in life. As I had told Waylon, I knew I would still have fears, I would still confront issues, and I would still have trouble building relationships. But I now felt I could handle all that. At the trauma center I had learned how to listen to my own voice, and I believed I had the strength I needed to build a future.

It was time to go home and get on with it.

CHAPTER SIX

A New House
and a New Love

I know in my heart I deserve to smile with you
for the rest of my life . . .

ART OF CREATING a new future, I think, is to be brave enough to deal with things in the past that just don't work for you anymore—and, if you have to, to leave them behind. I had begun doing that even before I went to the trauma center.

For example, I had given family members an ultimatum: act like a loving family or forget it. Prove that you're family by acting the way families should act, not by trying to get something out of me, and we'll talk. Otherwise, good-bye.

Perhaps the most dramatic example that sums up that break with the past was when I officially and legally changed my name. I put the wheels in motion just about a year after we were rescued, around the time *Finding Me* was published. The author of that book had lived a life I could never separate myself from, but it was a life I certainly wanted to put behind me. A new future deserved a new name, and I chose one that reflected my love and my hopes: Lily for the flowers that brighten my life; Rose to honor the kindness my friend's mother showed a lost little girl, me; and Lee, my son's middle name, to honor him, the best thing in my life up to this point.

It turns out that changing your name is not that hard to do. In fact, my lawyer handled the whole thing, organizing most of the paperwork and appearing on my behalf at the hearing before a judge. I didn't need to do a thing. In theory, the judge could have denied me the right to change my name—if I didn't have an acceptable reason. But I certainly did, and the hearing did not last long. I was Michelle Knight when it started, and I was Lillian Rose Lee when it ended—a new name for a new life.

My decision to write my own account of my captivity rather than to team up with Gina and Amanda in a joint writing project was another break with my past life. But it was not the kind of rupture some people thought it was. The main reason I decided to write my own book was that there were differences in what happened to each of us in Castro's house, and different experiences make for different stories. I was the first one he kidnapped, I had no family looking for me or worrying about me, I was held the longest, and I was treated the worst. It made sense for me to tell my own story my way and for them to tell theirs their way. In *Finding Me,* that is what I did, and in *Hope,* that is what they did, alternating their voices.

But the bond the three of us share is and always will be unbreakable. None of us chose for the bond to be formed. Survival required it. We went through terrible torture and suffering *together*—particularly Gina and I, who shared a room and sometimes were actually chained together. A connection like that can never be forgotten; it's always there. But in a way, the same experience that bonded us now keeps us on separate paths. Once we were freed, I think we all felt the need to find our own way to healing. We're all individuals, with our own personalities, our own character, and, of course, our own feelings. And we each need our own space.

The last time all three of us were together was in February 2014, when the governor of Ohio, John Kasich, honored

us with the state's Courage medals. We traveled to Medina
for the event at the Performing Arts Center. We heard the
governor praise our "inner strength and courage" in "staying
strong and sticking together." And we received a standing
ovation that seemed to go on forever. There was no need for
us to say much to one another, and we didn't. But we hugged
each other tight, and we all know we wish each other well.

I had a much different break with the past in mind when
I came back from Tennessee and the trauma center. One was
to break up with a guy I had been dating for a short while. It
hadn't been easy for me to begin dating, both because of my
trust issues with men and because of all the travel. I didn't
have much time to get to know someone well. But certainly
trust was the first stumbling block. I tried to overcome my re-
luctance because I didn't want my past to affect me forever.
I didn't want it to keep me from ever talking to a man—or
from ever thinking about having a relationship with a man.
So when I met "Pete," as I'll call him, at the Corner Alley, I
was at least open to talking with him. And in the beginning
at least, I was flattered by his attention. Yet we had only been
going out for a few weeks when I began to get the sense that
he was a very controlling person. Possessive too, always wanting to know where I was, who I was with, what I was doing.
As you can imagine, that did not go down well with me, and
after just a few weeks—before we ever formed a real relationship at all—I simply told him that it wasn't working out for
me and that we needed to go our separate ways.

Besides, a while before, some friends on Facebook had told me about a friend of theirs on Facebook they thought I might like. I checked him out and thought he seemed very handsome in his photos. I liked what he said in his posts and in his responses to other posts. He struck me as soft and sweet, not disrespectful or angry, as so many people on Facebook seem to be. Also, his posts and photos showed him to be a guy who honored his family, especially his mother, and I thought that was great too.

But you know how these things go: I wondered if he really looked like his photo and if my Facebook first impression of him would turn out to be accurate. So at first I didn't do anything about getting in touch with him. All I pretty much knew about him was that his name was Miguel.

I WAS READY to move on—and *so* ready to move out of my apartment! The truth is that I had been ready for some time. Only a few months of living downtown made me realize it wasn't right for me. The area was way too busy. I couldn't deal with the fast pace and constant activity.

I needed new surroundings and new friends. I knew I was drinking too much, still relying a little bit on alcohol to numb the memories that kept darting across my brain. It was hard not to, given the crowd I was running with. I was kind of tired of that crowd anyway. I still loved Jim and Kenny, still loved to meet up with Anita and Erna and go out on the town, but I was tired of those people I've described as "friends to my face but not behind my back."

What's more, the apartment management was giving me a hard time about having a dog, which I desperately wanted. First, they said no pets allowed at all; then they said it would be okay to have a small dog. *How small?* I wondered. Being limited in the number or size of pets just wasn't my style at all.

Also, I was still being noticed as a "celebrity" just about everywhere I went in Cleveland. Even after a year I couldn't walk down the street without people staring at me or stopping to ask if they could take a photograph. I felt I was being constantly watched and almost constantly judged. I had the sense that there were eyeballs on my back at all times.

Even all the traveling I had done for the book tour, although it opened new worlds to me, emphasized for me how much I wanted a home. I just wanted a peaceful place with a fenced-in yard where I could have dogs that could run free and I could walk out my back door in a bathing suit and *not* feel eyeballs on me.

My lawyer had found a real estate agent for me to work with, and off I went. We focused on a quiet, leafy suburb west of downtown Cleveland. I loved the first house I saw because it really looked like it was right in the forest, but it was carpeted from top to bottom, and I am totally allergic to anything except hypo-allergenic carpet. The minute I walked in, I started breaking out in hives. Obviously, ripping out all the carpets and maybe putting in all new flooring would take a lot of work, a lot of time, and a lot of money. Besides, you can't buy the very first house you see, can you? I decided to keep looking.

The next house I saw had chains attaching the light fixtures to the walls and ceilings. Chains are an obvious trigger for me—and a terrible one. I got out of there pronto. Another house I looked at had a basement just like Castro's, and I made a hasty retreat out of there as well.

I liked the next house a lot except for the color. It was kind of—pardon the expression—puke-green. Again, to repaint the whole outside would take time and money and, because it was already late fall, would probably have to wait until spring. I kept looking.

The next house had carpet in only a couple of places; I figured I could pull that up myself. It had a basement, but this one didn't seem to bother me. All it really needed was a fence around the backyard. I found myself thinking about how I would make this house my own, so I made an offer, and, as everyone does, I waited.

Do you remember what it was like to buy your first house? Or if you never have, can you imagine how thrilling it would be? I was in my apartment, which was looking less and less appealing every day, and when the real estate agent called to tell me that my offer on the house had been accepted, I was ecstatic. I looked around at my apartment and almost said, "Bye bye" out loud. The deal was closed just a few weeks before Thanksgiving, and I moved in—just around Thanksgiving 2014.

To me it was exciting enough to watch the fence go up. I was super-excited to move in all my furniture from the apartment, everything matching everything else, *and* go out and buy some more, *and* spend my first night in my own bed in my own bedroom in my very own home. And it was more than exciting to get to work fixing up the whole place my way. I did a lot of the work myself, with help from the local landscaper, a guy named Shawn, who became a friend. We ripped out the little bit of carpet to find beautiful hardwood floors underneath; all they needed was some sanding and refinishing where they had warped or buckled. And we painted the rooms different colors—one sky blue, one peach, one orange, one forest green. For the living room I chose a vibrant red color for the walls. That's when I got a lesson in how difficult it is to match red paint from bucket to bucket for big spaces. By the time we got to the second bucket, the mix was already shifty, and the whole wall began to look like a bunch of red patches. *Forget this,* I decided, and we painted the wall a creamy tan color that reminded me of the paper we got to draw on in kindergarten.

But soon after I moved in, as I was doing the various fixes and changes I had set my heart on, I began to notice the flaws. The first time it rained, I identified the leaking hole in the roof—that needed to be fixed right away. The first really cold day, when I could see my breath in front of me and crystallized ice on the windows even though *the heat was on,* I knew I would have to replace all the windows as soon as the weather was warm enough to do so. There were problems

A drawing I made a few years ago of my younger self. I was a young child stuck in a spiderweb of pain. I didn't know how to get out or who to trust.

My sweetie and I sharing a toast to a beautiful day in Hawaii.

Me horseback riding in
Puerto Rico.

My love and me celebrating
Thanksgiving. We are truly
blessed to have each other in
our lives.

Enjoying scuba diving in Florida. I was conquering my fears at
the same time.

Sharing my special day with family and friends, when two hearts became one. *Courtesy of Richard A. Gluszek III*

Walking down the aisle with a man I'm proud to call my dad. *Courtesy of Richard A. Gluszek III*

The two of us sharing a moment of peace. *Courtesy of Richard A. Gluszek III*

Our wedding cake. *Courtesy of Richard A. Gluszek III*

My dad and me sharing a dance to our favorite song, "What a Wonderful World." *Courtesy of Richard A. Gluszek III*

Our favorite photo that we took in the backyard of his best man's grandmother's house. *Courtesy of Richard A. Gluszek III*

My love and me sharing a dance to our favorite song. We were thinking out loud about how we fell in love and how love works in mysterious ways. *Courtesy of Richard A. Gluszek III*

Enjoying the last few days of warm weather by listening to nature's music.

Finding time to seize the moment and be one with nature.

My sweetie trying to bottle-feed a puppy we found in our front yard a couple of days after we got married.

My fur babies watching a movie together.

Celebrating my birthday with family
and friends!

Christmas is staying warm with a cup of peppermint hot cocoa or pumpkin spice coffee. Sharing those moments with the ones who are closest to your heart!

with the chimney, problems with the pipes. When I started having trouble breathing every time I went into the basement, I realized there was mold there. It had apparently been cleaned up just enough while the house was being shown to potential buyers, and now it was back like crazy. I pulled out the wall panels myself with a claw hammer and some muscle power, and there it was—black mold growing up and down the walls. Another disaster that had to be fixed.

Clearly I would need to spend the spring of the year fixing up the various disasters in my house. But I made a vow that for my next house, wherever and whenever it would be, I would not move in until I knew everything was just so.

Despite all the problems, I was not unhappy in this house. I loved the area, liked my neighbors—well, most of them— and was definitely able to walk out the back door in my bathing suit without feeling lots of eyeballs on me.

But then one day I went down to the basement as usual. It was dark down there, and I was feeling my way to the light switch when I suddenly got a spooky feeling. That particular trigger, igniting the terror of the basement in Castro's house all over again, seemed to be back in a big way. Maybe it had never gone away. *That's it,* I thought. *I can't go down there by myself again, and maybe I just can't do basements anymore.*

IN A WAY, it is funny that I "met" Miguel on Facebook. I had been somewhat suspicious of Facebook when I first learned about it. That was when I was back at the hospice, and I remember the shock I felt at all the negativity on display there. By now what bothered me was how wide open people were about sharing their feelings and thoughts and ideas. That sort of thing didn't come at all naturally to me. I was a bit more cautious about opening up in that way to people I didn't know.

So in my early days on Facebook I was more an observer than an active participant. I rambled around on the site, sometimes adding friends I knew from other places. It took a while before I started adding friends I had never met before, before I finally realized this was a good way to meet people and maybe make new friends. And why not make new friends? Little did I know that with so many of these new friends, we were going to have great conversations and end up finding that we had things in common with each other and *liking* each other.

That was my attitude the night I friend-requested Miguel. I was living in the house by then, just sitting around in my bedroom one night, trying to find something interesting to watch on television. I couldn't find a thing, so I checked my phone for messages, then opened up Facebook and took another look at that good-looking guy I had come upon before I headed down to Tennessee. *Hey*, I thought, *why not have a conversation with this guy, who seems so sweet, and see where it goes? Maybe we can build a friendship. Maybe it will turn into something more positive for me. Let's do it*, I decided. *Let's see what happens.*

It is weird now, as I write this, to remember myself thinking those thoughts at that time. So much has happened since then.

From his point of view, as he told me later, he thought the friend request must be from an impostor. He couldn't figure out why someone he knew about from newspaper headlines would be contacting him. Then he realized that, if it really was the person in the headlines, we probably knew some people in common on Facebook. That might explain why I was friend-requesting him. But even that was weird, because the people we knew in common on Facebook were just "acquaintances," not real friends, so he too thinks it is weird that we actually managed to connect that way.

Weird or fate or just luck. If I had found something great to watch on television that night, or if he had decided I *was* an impostor and not worth answering, who knows if we would ever have connected? I don't even want to think about that.

And obviously, we did connect. I had to wait a couple of days to get a response to my friend request because he was working odd hours at that time, while I was on the road a lot, so we were on crazily different schedules. But once we did connect, we just started messaging one another about our lives.

We're both Cleveland natives, so we always had that in common, and we exchanged a bunch of photos on Facebook, and then after a while I really wanted to hear his voice, so I said to him, *I'm sick of texting. Can you give me your number? Let's call.*

I can barely remember what we said on that first phone call. Nothing very significant. I remember not being surprised that he had a deep, really manly voice—and I remember liking it. I still do. I asked about his work, and he told me all about his experience in the Navy and his job as a medical courier. He also talked about the kind of music he liked—mostly country and rock 'n' roll as well as rap that makes sense. We were on the phone for hours that night, just sharing basic stuff, likes and dislikes, thoughts and opinions, and it took off from there. Like I say, not an especially heavy conversation. It's not like I got off the phone and shouted *Awesome!* But it *was* awesome to connect so comfortably and so easily with this guy I hadn't ever clapped eyes on.

I define the connection between us as "spiritual." Even before we met in person or saw one another, we could talk endlessly about the similarity between our lives, about issues with family, about what and how we thought about the things we both considered important in life. We told each other about the dreams we had had as kids and the dreams we had now, we talked about values, we gossiped, and we talked about our ideas of fun.

But I think what really helped seal the deal was that, by accident, we met in person at a restaurant one night. I was there to celebrate a friend's birthday, and he was there to have dinner with some friends, but neither Miguel nor I had any idea the other was going to be in that place that night. In fact, I was on my way back from the ladies' room and he was on his way to the men's room, and I know I wasn't paying attention to anything at all when suddenly we just bumped into each other. The recognition was instantaneous, thanks to the photos. But still, we had talked so much that when we actually introduced ourselves, my reaction was, *Holy cow! You're not a catfish! You're actually real!*

Of course, you need to know about the reality TV show *Catfish* to understand why I was pretty much blown away when I met Miguel in person. Each episode of the show is about two people who start a relationship online and then meet in person. Sometimes one of the two turns out not to have been honest in describing himself or herself: that's a catfish. Sometimes both are catfish.

I think that when Miguel and I met at the restaurant that night we were both skeptical: Would the other one turn out to be the person we knew from talking on the phone hour after hour? Or would one or both of us be lying about ourselves? We were both relieved to discover the other was absolutely real, but our relationship still continued as a phone friendship for several weeks.

I know he thought I was naïve about a lot of things—the things that I had missed during eleven years as a captive in Castro's house, the same way I had missed the TSA prohibition against liquids in your suitcase when you fly. He was very sweet and very patient about explaining those things to me: tablets, Instagram, Candy Crush—all sorts of stuff.

Of course, like everyone in Cleveland, he knew the basic facts about what had happened to the three of us in Castro's house. But he never tried to push me into talking about what happened to me, as many people do. He made me feel very comfortable, and so in time I did open up to him. I told him about my childhood, about how I felt that both my parents abused me in different ways, and about the trauma of what I went through in Castro's house. I waited a couple of weeks before I showed him a picture of my book, *Finding Me.* And I told him, "If you ever find the time, you can read a little bit of it."

I loved his reply. He said, "I prefer not to. I would rather get to know you." I thought that was very sweet. He knew who I was. He wasn't going to rush me. I was struck by how gentle and kind he was.

I tried to take it slow in talking about my life. I waited for him to tell me that what he was hearing had gotten too hectic for him and that I had to slow down. "We have to do this in pieces," he said to me. I realized that it was hard for him to process, hard for anyone to process. And I agreed we would take it slow.

In this way, our trust in one another grew and our affection deepened over time. By the time we got around to having our first actual date—by pre-arrangement, at a Thai restaurant, just the two of us on a cold January night in 2015—each of us was pretty sure we had found our soul mate. We just wanted to make sure it was real, and we were prepared, as I said, to "take it one day at a time and see where we go."

The dinner was both romantic and matter-of-fact. The question was: Are we a couple? The answer was: Of course! Why not?

IT ISN'T like I had never been in love before. I had been madly in love with Joey's father, Erik. In fact, one of the things I am particularly eager to tell my son when we do meet in person is that he was most definitely conceived in love. I may not have any idea what has become of Erik or where he is, but I know for certain that he and I were crazy about each other, enough so to defy bigots all around us who did not think a black boy and a white girl should be together.

But I was seventeen back then, and being madly in love wasn't something that lasted forever. This, with Miguel, was different.

For one thing, I was older. I had been through a lot, obviously. I had survived a level of trauma that I have been told would have driven some people crazy and some people to take their own life. I had bent but had not broken.

I wasn't optimistic about finding love after all I had been through. The whole world had heard the story of how I had been damaged by a filthy older man; even I wondered: Who would ever want me after that? How could anyone ever love me? I didn't see how it could happen. But that didn't mean I didn't want to be loved. Everybody wants to be loved. I opened myself up to the possibility, and it happened. Miguel happened. He didn't judge me for my past. He understood that the past had been done *to* me. He looked beyond that and saw who I really am—me. And he found what he saw beautiful.

As we sat at dinner in the Thai restaurant that night, we knew this wasn't going to be an easy transition. There were practical reasons: he was a mostly nine-to-five guy, and I was on the road all the time giving talks and presentations. And there were deeper reasons: neither of us had ever made this kind of commitment before. But it just seemed right.

So in the early part of 2015 Miguel moved in. And over the next weeks and months our relationship had a chance to grow stronger and more rewarding day after day. We kept our relationship quiet for a while. Miguel's close friends knew about us and were glad for him. Although not everybody felt that way, with every passing day we were more and more sure about what we had.

The first time I met his family wasn't easy. I had met his sister first, but this time the whole extended family was there, at his uncle's house, and that meant a large number of relatives. Miguel's family is originally from Puerto Rico, so an abundance of warmth gets spread around at a family gathering. There were a lot of people there, and I think Miguel and I both felt we were a little bit on exhibit—I know I did. I had some delightful and pleasant conversations with some of the family and hit some very awkward moments with others. Somebody said to me, "You know, you can always go buy a baby." That made me pull back hard; it was such a thoughtless thing to say. Another person joked that Miguel was "out for your money." I didn't find that funny at all. I really wanted to leave, but Miguel said we had to hang on a bit longer, so I just stayed silent and focused on the food, a selection of Spanish dishes that seemed to go on forever.

Miguel had warned me that his family was not all that affectionate. "Growing up," he said, "it was tough love." I guess neither of us got the family we would have liked as kids. So it meant even more to us that we now had each other.

Miguel is a quiet man. People around him can get boisterous and noisy, like when his whole family gets together, and he always manages to be calm. When you're one on one with Miguel, he does not waste a lot of words and he means what he says. But the first time he told me I was beautiful, I had trouble believing him. I had always been told I was ugly. I had been bullied for being short, for my weight, my clothes, my hair. I had been called names that made fun of my looks. But when Miguel said the words, "You're so beautiful," I began to realize that he was talking about the me he saw deep inside. That was the me I hoped I was and wanted to be. *If he could see that,* I thought, *maybe it's true. Maybe I really am beautiful. Maybe I do deserve to be loved.*

Physical intimacy didn't happen right away, mostly because I had to let it develop on its own terms and at its own pace. We took it slow—getting close was a process. I felt the need to explain to Miguel that I had some issues. I had some fears that any intimacy might feel like what Castro had done to me, what others had done to me. We waited; we took our time. When it did happen, I realized I didn't have anything to fear. The experience was entirely different. What made the difference was love.

And love is a two-way street. If he could see into the corners of my soul, I was aware of a certain darkness in him in those first months of our relationship. I knew that he was drinking every day and was having trouble controlling it. We talked about it. We both knew it was a problem. But that's what alcohol can do to you: it controls *you* instead of the other way around. It all came to a head in the late fall of 2015.

We threw a Halloween party that year, and the next day Miguel woke up sick. Not just hungover sick, but really, really sick—sweating and shivering, with a 103-degree fever and his complexion turning gray. We rushed to the hospital. By the time we arrived, Miguel was barely responding. I was afraid I was going to lose him.

The doctors diagnosed a viral infection that had inflamed Miguel's lymph nodes. But a deeper and more significant issue, revealed in a series of tests, was that his liver had been affected. Miguel spoke frankly to the doctors about his past alcohol abuse, how he would quit drinking, then start up again, time after time. With each "new" period of drinking, his tolerance level rose, so he would drink more. Over time that can be poisonous. What had brought him to the hospital, we realized, was not the drinking itself but his body telling him that he was poisoning himself. In a way, his body was saving his life by stopping in its tracks for a while.

A long while. Miguel was in the hospital nearly a month. I was there with him night and day. I canceled a number of speaking engagements and slept in a chair. I remembered what it is like to be alone in a hospital when you don't really know what's wrong with you. So I stayed.

Finally, one of the doctors told us the truth flat out. "If you don't change the way you live," this doctor told Miguel, "you'll have cirrhosis of the liver within five years." Miguel knew well what that meant: a relative of his had died of that disease. He made a vow to change his drinking habit.

It wasn't easy. In fact, the change was pretty stressful. There were days when he would get what he called his "Damn I want a beer" feeling. But he didn't give in. He stuck it out, tough as it was. And I was with him every step of the way. Today Miguel's drinking consists of maybe a glass of wine on special occasions—and he mostly doesn't finish it. I am so proud of him for beating this problem. As for me, I like a glass of wine each evening, and that's it.

WE DECIDED we needed a vacation—a break from what we had been through over the past several months and a change of scenery. It was very nearly winter, but we rented a cabin in the Great Smoky Mountains, about as beautiful a place as there is and a great way to escape city life, which is just what we did.

One evening I noticed that instead of turning on the light switch, Miguel had set out candles instead. Also, he had tuned the radio to some soft, romantic music. And then he got down on his knees. "Honey," he said, "don't be mad at me. I had planned to surprise you and propose to you, but"—he hesitated, then burst out—"I grabbed the wrong bag and left the ring at home!"

My heart was so full of love for him and excitement for us both that I couldn't say a word. Miguel went on: "But I still want to do this," he said.

So, still on his knees, he did. He told me that he could not see his life without me in it and that he wanted me to be a part of his life forever.

"Will you marry me?" he asked.

You know I did not hesitate, did not skip a beat. "Yes," I said. "I will."

The thing I once thought could never happen for me had happened: love, and now marriage. To me it all seemed most definitely official: everything you need for getting engaged except the ring. And really, why do you need a ring anyway?

FAST FORWARD to the day of Christmas Eve back home in Cleveland. I had been to a movie with a friend and came home to hear from Miguel that the dogs had torn up our Christmas tree and made a mess of all the ornaments.

I just groaned. Christmas is one of my favorite times of year, and it was frustrating to think it had gotten messed up. That's the word Miguel had used: mess. So I walked into the living room to see just how big the mess was.

"Where's the mess?" I asked Miguel.

"You have to get closer," he said.

I moved closer to the tree. "Where?" I said. I couldn't see any ornaments at all.

"Closer," Miguel said.

Then I saw that one of my favorite ornaments, a little Baby Jesus, had been knocked off the tree onto the track of the little railroad that goes around our Christmas tree. I looked closer. Still closer. And I saw that Baby Jesus was holding a ring.

I burst into tears. Couldn't help it.

"Lily Rose Lee, will you marry me?" Miguel asked again.

I was crying too hard to talk, so for an answer I put the ring on. It fit perfectly.

We were now totally "officially engaged." We could even set the date for our wedding. By my choice, it would be May 6, 2016, the third anniversary of my rescue, the start of me being "reborn" as Lily Rose Lee. Because it was now Christmas 2015, that meant we had less than five months to plan everything.

CHAPTER SEVEN

Marriage and Home

My new beginning with you is a blessing . . .

S TARTING WHEN I was about twelve years old or so, I had these big, beautiful daydreams about the wedding I would have one day. Because the dreams were all in my head, it was easy for everything about the event to be perfect. There would be huge bouquets of flowers, the groom would be handsome, I would look gorgeous in my long, white bridal gown, and everything at the reception would just sparkle. All the guests who attended the wedding would be warm, loving friends and family members, and all of us would have a wonderful time and feel happy and glad for days and weeks afterward.

I don't know how this idea got planted in my brain. I had never been to such a wedding, and I certainly had never seen a happy marriage—not anywhere in my family anyway. But I guess the idea that there could be a good marriage and a beautiful wedding to celebrate it must have just been in the air. And like a lot of little girls of twelve or so, I plucked it out of the air and made it my own fantasy.

Later, during the years I was a captive in Castro's house, as soon as he let me have a piece of pencil and some paper, I even designed the wedding dress for that perfect wedding: white, of course, strapless, floor length, and with long sleeves that I thought added a real touch of elegance. I was no longer a little girl by that time, but my little-girl dream was still in my head, and I drew the dress in great detail, over and over: the perfectly beautiful dress I would wear as a bride at my perfectly beautiful wedding. When you're confined and have nothing to do with your time except wait to be abused, imagining the details of a wedding that will never happen is a good way to pass the time. It's a survival strategy: Focus on the impossible. Imagine something so far-fetched it can take your mind away from the reality. And you never want to think about the reality because it's unbearable.

As the years went by, I was able to get hold of papers or magazines so I could also clip out different news stories or photos that depicted what I wanted such a wedding to look like. I could add and subtract, change and edit all the details of this fantasy: These are the flowers I would like. . . . This is the tablecloth. . . . These are the dresses I want my brides-maids to wear. . . . This is what I want the church to look like. It all got grander and grander, further and further away from the reality of life in that house.

And then it became real, and I was actually planning my own wedding with Miguel. By then, of course, my ideas had changed somewhat.

I don't have to tell you that weddings are big business and a big deal, and the options available, not to mention all sorts of possible added luxuries, are enough to make you dizzy. I realized how easy it is to drink the Kool-Aid and plan a cele-bration that is over the top in a million ways, with flowers or ropes of twinkling lights hanging from the ceiling, rose pet-als six inches deep spread over the aisle you walk down, and, for all I know, a private airplane waiting to take you to your honeymoon. The bride and groom could get lost in all that, and I just wasn't interested in it at all. I didn't want our wed-ding to be about luxury or glitz; I just wanted the day to be a celebration of the fact that Miguel and I were committing ourselves to one another. We were joining our lives together, and a celebration of our union would not need a lot of doo-dads or trinkets or extras. But it would need some basics, and those basics had to be perfect: the flower arrangements, the dress, loving friends and family we cared about as our guests, and each other.

One very important thing we also needed was privacy— mine and Miguel's and that of the friends and family members we invited.

Privacy had become an increasingly serious issue to me and a very important concern. Whether I liked it or not, whether I asked for it or not, I was a public figure. My public status didn't just come from the fact that I was one of the "famous" three women who had escaped the captivity of Ariel Castro's house; I also now regularly made speeches and presentations and carried out advocacy on the subjects of domestic violence and abuse. That too kept me in the public eye.

As part of that work I also had a presence on social media, and as everybody knows, putting yourself out there on social media can be a great thing, but it can have its downside as well. For me the downside was sometimes unpleasant. Even two years after my rescue and almost a year after my book, *Finding Me*, was published, the unpleasant downside had been happening a lot, and sometimes it was scary.

The comments people posted could be really ugly. We all know that it is pretty easy to mouth off on Facebook.

Many people posted mean and disgusting comments—even hateful—and some people used the site to post sometimes threatening comments. Awful things like, "I hope you die" were pretty upsetting, and you just have to wonder why people decide it is okay to post such terrible thoughts.

I could tell myself to avoid comments like that or try to put them out of my mind, although that wasn't always easy. I was fair game. What was really hard to deal with were things like people posting photos of me on Facebook—photos I didn't know anything about and hadn't given anyone permission to shoot, much less post on the internet. There would also be posts that said where I had been seen or where I was going to show up. Posts like that made me very uncomfortable. I felt as if I were being watched and, even worse, like I needed to hide myself away.

They could criticize me or praise me up and down, they could question what I told audiences or my motives, but when they used the internet to threaten, that was getting into a whole different territory. I realized that the talks I gave and the advocacy I pursued were my business—my profession—and I decided I needed to take a more professional and businesslike approach to my privacy and even my security.

I had had a relationship with a lawyer ever since my rescue, and she had helped me a lot in making sure I got the care I needed and deserved, in getting me on my feet financially, and in guiding me through the process of writing a book and going on a book tour. Now it seemed to be time for a different kind of lawyer to ensure that I was getting the privacy protection I needed in contract arrangements being made on my behalf. So I hired a lawyer who was an expert in legal guidelines for privacy issues, and at about the same time I signed on with a public relations firm that could make sure that the stories and messages I wanted to share got out to the public clearly and in the right way. Along with the agency that sets up my speaking engagements, these professionals make up my business "team," and I am totally grateful to them for their help in keeping my business affairs safe and private.

My attorney and PR team helped with the wedding too. I suppose a lot of people feel conflicted, as I did, about "publicizing" their wedding. In a way you want the world to know, and in a way you want it to be just about the two of you. I wanted our wedding to be just my and Miguel's moment that we would share, celebrate, and enjoy with close friends of our choosing, and I didn't want it to be something the wider world posted about or talked about or even knew about. We also wanted to be absolutely sure that the guests wouldn't disclose anything about the event ahead of time, and we didn't want anybody posting photos or sharing details about it afterward. The wedding was for us. It wasn't a public event.

But as anyone who has ever staged a wedding knows, even a simple wedding takes a lot of preparation and planning, and a lot of preparation and planning means a lot of details. And details, unfortunately, are the kind of thing that can leak out without your being aware of it. So I was glad to have my team's help in making sure people wouldn't suspect ahead of time what was going on. We didn't want anyone leaking to the press that there might be a wedding in store for one of the three well-known Cleveland women rescued from captivity just two years before. My name change helped, but we still had to exercise caution.

Even so, the day before the wedding some woman texted me on Facebook Messenger: "I wish you were dead." Why she wanted me dead I do not know, nor do I have any idea what sets any of these people off. I reported the message to my PR team, and they took over monitoring my Facebook page and Messenger. I didn't need to see such stuff, and I was glad someone else was checking on it. And certainly, for a day that was supposed to be nothing but joy, I was relieved that my team had my back.

As if planning a wedding wasn't enough, Miguel and I chose this time to sell my house and buy a new house for our life together. We were sitting around one night figuring out what it was going to cost us to make all the needed repairs in the house we were in.

"The roof will probably be the biggest expense," I said.

"We should fix the chimney at the same time," said Miguel. "By the way, did you know that the 'automatic' garage door isn't so automatic anymore? I had to open and close it manually twice today. That's another repair job."

"The first thing I want handled is that mold in the basement," I put in. "That's a complete remediation job, and it won't be cheap."

I think we both sort of looked at each other as if we were having the same thought at the same time: What more can go wrong? I'm the one who said it: "Honey, I just can't take it anymore. Let's find a house that is just for us, with problems we can fix ourselves, and just sell this one as is."

And that's what we did.

We realized it was a little bit crazy to do these three pretty substantial things all at once—sell a house, buy a house, have a wedding—and we did think we might just lose our heads, but we decided to take things one day at a time, and the truth is: it worked.

We already had a buyer for our house—Shawn, the landscaper guy who knew all the pitfalls he would be facing when he took over from us. He was also good enough to extend the deadline that new owners usually set for the sellers to get out of the house. That meant that we could take a little more time than is normally available to find the house we wanted and to move in. We had barely gotten started when I had to go off to the Cayman Islands for a speaking engagement at a conference of people who work with victims of domestic abuse and sexual assault. This turned out to be a really important trip for me because I learned about One Safe Place, an organization that offers intervention services and safety to such victims and helps them get back on their feet. This trip planted in my brain the idea of creating a similar transition center where victims of the kind of abuse I had known could go to feel safe and get the kind of services that empower them to be able to take care of themselves: health insurance, education, job training, and more.

Miguel called while I was down in the Caymans and, out of the clear blue sky, said he was texting me photos of a house he thought I would absolutely love—"the house for us," he called it. Remembering my experience with my first house, which looked great on the outside but turned out to have one problem after another, I asked Miguel, "Did you check it out to make sure everything was all right?"

"I'm doing that now," he said.

Then he texted me a bunch of photos of the house, and oh my gosh, it was gorgeous. I fell in love with the kitchen first—stone floor, wood cabinets, granite countertops—and then with the backyard, with its wonderful deck. In fact, this house had everything we were looking for. "This is it," I told my sweetie. When I got home, as soon as I got over being sick with some bug I had caught, we went to see the house and decided to make an offer. By the time I was ready to walk down the aisle, on May 6, 2015, the second anniversary of my rescue and rebirth, the house was ours.

Back from the Caymans, I was also ready to get serious about wedding preparations. I finally sat down and called the David's Bridal near me to make an appointment for checking out wedding dresses, making sure first that they could handle arrangements to safeguard my privacy at the same time.

The dress: finding the right one was work—hot, sweaty work as I tried on at least thirty different gowns until I found the one I wanted. Even then, the dressmakers practically had to rebuild the whole thing to match the design I had worked on all those years as a child and in Castro's house. First it was too long, then the fix made it too short. It was really hard to get the bodice just right. I wanted the flare of the skirt more fitted, the ruffle less bunched up, and the train more swirly. The butt had to be tailored just right, and the underlying bustier had to be tighter. In the end the gown was so reworked underneath that it was pretty heavy to wear, although once I started heading down the aisle, I forgot all about it.

But the dress was just the beginning. Ever try finding the perfect wedding venue in May? I think it may be tougher than finding a venue for June. My first choice would have been the Botanical Gardens, but that was out of the question: booked solid with birthday parties, graduation parties, and, of course, weddings. Then I would have loved to be married in an area in the park near the Cleveland Zoo, in a beautiful small venue where we could feel we were surrounded by animals. But after much consideration, we decided the cost was too high; we would be busting our budget before we even got started on our life together, so we had to make another choice.

Jim, a taxi driver by trade, drove me around from place to place between his work assignments, and that was how we found the Western Reserve Historical Society, which is a pretty amazing institution in Cleveland with all sorts of important artifacts showing the history of Northeast Ohio. The

Western Reserve, in case you don't know, is something that goes way back in American history to the time of the original thirteen colonies. The King of England granted this huge piece of land to the colony of Connecticut—until Connecticut sold it in 1800. A few years later the land was first surveyed by a guy named Moses Cleaveland, which is how my hometown got its name (after dropping the "a" and turning "Cleaveland" into Cleveland). The Historical Society was a perfect venue for us because some of its most important collections contain things we particularly love. There is art, of course, and all sorts of antiques, including its very famous collection of antique cars—which go from the earliest automobiles of the 1890s right through to the cars of today. Both Miguel and I love antiques, and I particularly love art, while he particularly loves cars. So the venue "covered" our favorite things. My son, Joey, also loved toy cars when he was a little boy, so I could feel he was with us too. It made the museum the right choice for our reception.

For the ceremony we chose the nondenominational Church of God in Elyria, Ohio, just about a half-hour drive from the Historical Society. We chose that church because they welcome everyone—whatever you look like, whatever you like to wear, however you like to worship—and because we love the pastor, Chad Britt, and his very sweet wife and daughter.

But I was in charge of every detail so I could match the dream wedding in my head, revised from the dream I had at the age of twelve, as closely as possible. I wanted the color of the bridesmaids' dresses to match the color of a bluish-purple hydrangea found for me by my friend Kimberly, who does flowers, and I wanted the lilies in my wedding bouquet to match that color too, so the bouquet would consist of the hydrangea-colored lilies, pink roses, and white carnations. That wasn't easy. I had to bring one of the bridesmaids' dresses into the flower shop even before they had been fitted on the four bridesmaids to try to find a matching color, but what we finally figured out was to dip the flowers, petal heads down, in purple hair dye, pull them out, and wash them off. That worked.

The dresses themselves were *almost* a disaster. One of my bridesmaids sent a photo of herself in the dress sent to her, and I had to message her back that it looked like a garbage bag on her—way too big. So there was a bit of backing and forthing before the four ladies got their dresses just right.

The flowers, with their difficult-to-match color, arrived April 1 and had to be made not just into bouquets for me and the bridesmaids but also into arrangements at the church and at the reception as well as into boutonnieres for the groomsmen.

I made a special pillow for the ring bearer to carry, a little boy named Robbie. He was normally a demon of energy, but I was sure he would behave himself beautifully on the wedding day. (He did!)

I picked all the decorations for the church and for the reception too. I chose the menu, which was going to feature Puerto Rican specialties like pork with rice and beans, empanadas, fish, and chicken. I wanted a vanilla wedding cake with lemon meringue filling and a butter-cream white frosting to set it all off, and that is precisely what the cake lady made for me—to perfection. The cake would sit atop a gazebo-like construction with smaller cakes on stands around it. There were two wedding rings on the top of the cake, and they were a last-minute substitution because the item I originally ordered to crown the cake—a porcelain bride and groom in dance pose surrounded by a heart—didn't arrive until long after the event. I guess every wedding has a few "hiccups," as Miguel called them, but although the rings were a late-hour fix, they looked beautiful. Underneath the main cake and sort of inside the gazebo was a self-contained little waterfall of lemon "wine," as we called it—nonalcoholic so our nondrinking guests could enjoy it too.

The event took a lot of planning, offered a lot of choices to consider, required making a lot of decisions, and was altogether a lot of work. So as the wedding itself grew closer, I was more and more ready to quit work and have some fun. And that was what the bachelorette party was all about.

I should say my bachelorette *parties*, because we had two events on two separate days. One event was when my friends and I went to a comedy club together. The problem was that the comedian wasn't very funny at all, but what was hilarious was all of us at our table making jokes about the unfunny comedian and my friends closing in tight around me trying to keep me hidden from prying eyes. We laughed so hard that we were crying. The second event was a paint-and-sip party, one of my favorite things, where the painting assignment was to create a skyline with a forest in the background, a mountain of a different color, and in the front a boat with two people in it—either a man and a woman or your best friend and you. The painting alone took four hours and was just wonderful. Somebody brought me a drink in a martini glass with rainbow sprinkles around the rim. The drink itself contained alcohol plus more alcohol diluted with bubbly. It was awesome. It was also pretty much a lethal weapon. What a great pair of parties!

(Yes, there was a bachelor party too, but of course I did not attend and have no idea what happened there . . .)

THE WEDDING DAY itself started for me at eight in the morning, when I went to get my hair done, then to get my nails done, then to get my makeup applied. The makeup, done at Macy's, was the last stop. After all that, I was just a bit late getting to the church, where my dress awaited me. My final choice, after trying on all those possibilities, was pretty much the very dress I had designed years before. It was strapless, floor length, and pure white. All that was missing were the long sleeves I had drawn in my design, and I was just as glad. Sleeves would have been "too much" and too warm, and this way I got to show off some of my tattoos.

Was I nervous? Yes. Butterflies were flapping their wings like crazy inside my stomach. I was excited beyond belief. If

I had never even thought I would ever find love, I certainly never ever thought I would have this day—a beautiful wedding with the people I cared about around me and with all the special touches and all the trimmings I had dreamed about as a kid. My four bridesmaids in their deep-purple dresses and the four groomsmen in black suits with deep-purple ties and vests led by best man Tony, Miguel's close friend from work, completed the picture I had carried in my head for years. Yes, it had been a little weird to have to get dressed in secret in a room of the church—I felt like I was hiding, which I didn't like. But my thoughts were on what came next.

I certainly must have seemed nervous to the pastor. "You sure you want to go through with this?" he asked me jokingly. "I can open the back door for you if you'd like to escape." Nothing was further from my mind, but laughing at the joke was just what I needed to break the tension and settle down a bit. I looked down the aisle of the very simple church—white peaked ceiling, chairs instead of pews, a plain altar and a wooden cross and Pastor Chad and Miguel standing there, and suddenly it was as if I were the homecoming queen at all those high school weekends I never attended or the belle of the ball at the high school proms I had never gone to—all rolled into one. All eyes were on me, and all I could hear was a deep silence.

Then the person I call Dad, my dear friend Jim, lifted my veil and said, "You ready?" I took a deep breath, tried to forget about the weight of the dress, told myself to get rid of my fears about tripping on my walk down the aisle, and nodded.

Jim took my hands and looked into my eyes lovingly, and we started down the aisle.

My worries about my high heels evaporated. I felt as if I were floating on air. I could hear people say under their breath, "You look gorgeous," "Hey, it's perfect," "You go, girl." The love I felt for the people around me and the love I sensed coming from them was almost overwhelming. All that emotion lifted me up so high that I felt like I was gliding down the aisle to my sweetie, so handsome in his white tux—his "monkey suit," as he called it—with a pink vest and pink tie that matched the flowers in my bouquet. And he was crying. He couldn't help it, and here is what he wrote later about that moment: "The joy of seeing my wife coming down the aisle looking so beautiful made the beast inside me cry and feel like his heart had just bowed. I had tried hard not to lose a tear, but I just didn't seem to have the strength to not do so. So, I lost it then and let the tears flow as she approached."

Jim stepped to the side, and Miguel took my hand, and the first thing we all did was say a prayer of praise and thanks to God that we were all here. Then my sweetie and I recited our vows, each of us to the other, and I could hear some people crying, some sighing, some saying "Amen." Whispered words of love floated up to the front of the church. "You deserve this," I heard someone say. "She is so strong," said another. I knew I was in the right place at the right time. I knew this was my moment. What I had dreamed about at twelve had come true in a way I could never have imagined, and all I felt was love.

The time came for us to exchange rings, and here was another wedding "hiccup." The ring Miguel slid onto my finger was too big—it swam on me. The ring I put on Miguel's finger was too small—it only went as far as his knuckle. Somebody—either the ring people or I myself—had gotten the two sizes reversed. At the time the mistake just seemed sweet, and of course everything got fixed later.

One of the most touching moments of the wedding was when my sweetie and I each held our own candles, lit a single candle together, and then blew out our individual candles. As we blew them out, the smoke made an image of an angel in the background. We both noticed it at the same moment. Neither of us knew it would happen. We looked at one another, and we both just felt: *Wow.*

The pastor pronounced us husband and wife, and it was done. I was a married woman, something I had dreamed about but never thought I would become. It was time to celebrate, but first we wanted to take photos. We drove to the park we had chosen for just that purpose—a common background for Cleveland wedding pictures—and of course it was packed. A beautiful day in May had drawn crowds of people, children, and dogs. We didn't even get out of the cars. We figured we would just add to the commotion and would probably blow any cover of privacy we had hoped for. Best man Tony to the rescue: "I got a better idea," he said.

"Follow me to my grandmother's house. It's on the lake! Best background for wedding shots ever!"

He was right. The place was great, and so was Tony's grandmother, who insisted Tony open a bottle of wine so she could toast what she called "this special occasion." She toasted our "new beginning," and she wished us the strength to never let anything ever tear our love apart. I found her toast beautiful and, of course, was crying throughout. And we got some wonderful pictures against the background of our beautiful Lake Erie.

But when we got back in the car and headed toward our reception at the Historical Society, we hit another hiccup. The car had stopped at a gas station, and I happened to look at my phone, and on Facebook there was a picture taken at the wedding. The guy who took the photo had been a guest at the wedding and had signed a statement that he would not do what he had just done: post any photos on the internet. I was really irritated, so we got hold of the guy at once and made him take down the photo. Once that was done, I calmed down and was ready to get back to having a good time.

Of course, by now we were half an hour late for our own wedding reception, but we had vowed not to rush but to take our time. We meant to be creating memories with family and friends, and memories don't always get created on schedule. Our schedule wasn't perfect, but the memories were, and it's the memories that count. That's exactly what the party at the Historical Society was all about: memories we will always have.

Family members among the guests included Miguel's mother, sister, grandmother, some cousins, and some uncles. Attending from my biological family was Little Mikey, my aunt Paula's son, the little cousin I had taken care of for much of his life. Other of my "family" members were, of course, Anita and Erna, whom I consider my grandmother and my mom—not biologically, but those are the roles they have in my life—and, of course, Jim. In addition to these family members were all the good friends we had invited, and all were certainly in a mood to party.

We were in a great place for doing just that—in a rotunda, under a domed ceiling, in what felt to me like the perfect banquet hall but encircled by old airplanes and old cars and old bicycles—all part of the Historical Society's collection. The decorations at our table were gorgeous, just as I had imagined and planned. There were a few tiny discrepancies: some of our decorations got mixed up with decorations from the other event being held that day at the Historical Society, a Jewish bar mitzvah! But it didn't matter at all, and we just laughed. *We have each other*, we said to ourselves, *and that's all that matters.*

I had a ball. There were toasts, some that made me cry and some that made me laugh. My girlfriend Dawn made me laugh, and so did best man Tony, who ended his toast with the words, "May the force be with you!" That was when I found out that I had married a *Star Wars* fan.

Miguel's sister, Danielle, said the prayer before the meal, and then we all sat down and ate and ate and ate. We let the food settle for a bit as we took a little walk among the cars in the collection and had our photos taken sitting on the "horses" of the famous Grand Carousel, dating from 1905 and one of the treasures of the Historical Society. Jim and I were to sing a song together—the K-Ci & JoJo song "All My Life," in which they sing "Close to me you're like my father. . . . Close to me you're like my brother," which pretty much says how Jim and I are to each other: we're family, pure and simple. But Jim forgot the words, so I sang the song by myself, and I really sang it *to* him.

Miguel and I, of course, led out the dancing, and our first dance was to the Ed Sheeran song "We Found Love Right Where We Are." Slow and easy and very romantic—just the two of us, very much in the moment.

Jim and I danced too—to "What a Wonderful World." This time neither of us had to sing.

The party went on nearly until midnight. I was glad that everyone had a designated driver. We didn't go on a honeymoon just then—that waited until 2017, when we had a delayed honeymoon in Hawaii. After a wedding that was as wonderful as I had dreamed about and planned for, we very happily just went home.

A FEW MONTHS after the wedding of our dreams Miguel and I moved into the house of our dreams. We had sold most of our old furniture and bought new furniture to fit our new home and our new life. We made the place ours, with a pond out back and a fire pit that lets us sit outdoors most of the year, with room for the animals, with space for his man cave and space for me to paint and write, room for us to be ourselves and room for us to be together. It seemed to me that two years after my rescue, my "rebirth" was complete.

I had found "my sweetie," as I always call him, my other half, my soul mate. And we were sheltered together in a beautiful home. It was a totally new beginning.

CHAPTER EIGHT

Unfinished Business: Seeking My Roots, Planning My Future

What really matters is how you feel about yourself. Don't let anybody change your smile . . .

I THINK THERE ARE two ways to define *family*. One is your biological family—all the people related to you by blood or marriage: your mother and father, their mothers and fathers, and all of *their* ancestors going back generations—all the people you get your genes from.

Under that definition of family, I am pretty sure I know who my mother is, and I think I know who my father was, but I may never be entirely sure. I am convinced that I was never really told the truth at all about my father or my grandparents or any other of my blood relatives, so I never really knew who was who in my family and how each may truly have been related to me. And for a long time I thought, *If I don't know who I came from, how can I know who I am?* I also wondered why people wouldn't tell me the truth about my relatives.

But there is another definition of *family*. Family is the people who love you and care for you, who keep you safe when you are growing up, and who give you the tools you will need to go out into the world on your own and become the person you can be. Sometimes—most times, I think—this kind of family is also your biological family. But not always.

Not in my case. Growing up I never had a family like that second definition. In the house where I spent my childhood there was no love or caring that I could ever see. Certainly none I ever felt. Instead, there were different kinds of abuse. I didn't feel safe from any of it. Sometimes, when I was old enough, I would escape from my family and run to the house of my friend Carol. Her mother, Rose, took me in when she could and made me feel safe and loved. That was the only time I ever experienced what a family could and should be—from someone who was no blood relative at all. But what Rose showed me—the example she gave—was enough so that when I had a child of my own, I had an idea of mother love that I tried to follow.

I grew up believing I had two brothers. It was my job to get them up and dressed and out to school. My cousin also lived with us, and I took care of him too. And there was also a succession of what I was told were aunts, uncles, and other cousins. I wasn't sure how they were related.

The household was chaotic. I never knew who would be there or why they were there, just that they were all called "family" or "relatives" in some way. I was five when one of these "relatives" sexually abused me for the first time. Then he continued to abuse me, always threatening that if I told anyone, I wouldn't be believed, but he would kill me anyway.

Beatings often accompanied the sexual abuse, especially if I resisted or cried. And I got beatings for anything I did that could be considered an offense—not doing a chore, talking back, anything.

Along with the abuse was the drinking. It went on all day and all night. And the drugs. The household seemed to me to run on booze and weed—or much stronger stuff when they could get it.

The abuser in my family had always warned me never to tell about the abuse he inflicted. "Nobody will believe you," he said. "Nobody will listen to you." It seemed to me he was right. In first grade I was going to school covered in scratches and bruises. One day I was so tired of it that I told my teacher I was being hurt at home. My brothers, who were in a different school, told their teacher around the same time. We were assigned a social worker.

Nothing changed. Nothing happened. I don't know why. I have no idea what, if anything, the social worker did or the reasons why we were never rescued from our family. All I know is that the system failed me. It failed me in first grade, and it failed me every time after that when I tried to get help. In fact, I just got beaten up more and more. I have a clear memory of being beaten in my room after telling someone "in authority" that I was being hurt at home. I stood there screaming out loud with every hit I took, and I was praying for somebody to come rescue me. No one heard me; no one came to save me. I felt like I was all alone in the world. I was a kid, and I didn't understand why the world was so cruel or why no one seemed to believe that I was being abused.

Sometimes, after I told someone at school about what was happening at home, I was instructed to "bring my parents" in, and then I had to repeat my complaints in front of them. All that got me was another beating when we got back home. Not one teacher or guidance counselor or caseworker or doctor that I tried to tell about my abuse ever did anything about it.

My mother often kept me out of school, and sometimes, when I went to school, she came and hauled me out of class, claiming I had a doctor's appointment or a family wedding to go to or a family funeral. My teachers didn't notice or turned a blind eye to how far behind I was academically. It wasn't until I got to high school that I began learning. How? I taught myself—to read, to do math, everything. I had to. No one else—at school or at home—was teaching me anything except how powerless I was to control anything that happened to me. I always felt threatened, and I was always afraid.

By high school I had pretty much gotten used to the fact that my family was the way it was. The abuse was ongoing, and it seemed clear to me by then that no one in authority was going to do anything about it. I got to be an expert at covering up. I mean that in two ways. First, I managed to avoid most conversations about parents or family that teenage girls have—avoid them or detour away from them. The other girls were complaining that their parents didn't understand them or that they set curfews. My complaints would have been about abuse, so I kept quiet. Second, I also dressed in ways that would cover up my bruises and the scars of my own skin cutting. As ashamed as I was of the family I came from, I also didn't want to broadcast it to others.

That was what my family life was like when I was growing up. Through high school, through my pregnancy and the birth of my son, through trying to find some other place— some safe place—for me and Joey to live. Except for Carol and Rose, that was the only model of a family I ever knew. I had no idea there were any other ways to be a family, but I figured there had to be. I very much wanted to believe that every family *could* operate the way Carol and Rose did.

And for a long time I still wanted to know where I came from, who I came from, and what ethnic and racial identities run in my blood. I suppose it's natural to wonder about those things. Maybe we think that knowing what you come from will tell you something about yourself. Maybe we think it holds the key to some important knowledge that will give us some sense of power over how we act.

In my case, at the same time that I was working hard to put the past behind me, I still wanted to know more about where I came from. I was about to be married, after all, so I was about to form my own family with Miguel and, if possible, to have children with him. I thought it would be important to understand where and how I got the strength to survive what I survived, both at home from as early as I can remember and in Castro's house. I wanted to know who or what among my ancestors had the backbone I inherited that let me come out of a lifetime of abuse without becoming abusive myself. Where does my iron will come from? When and how did my ability to forgive get locked into my DNA?

Somebody or something way back when—probably a lot of somebodies and somethings—put into the genetic mix the qualities that add up to me. I was curious to know who or what they were.

So I tried to find out. I once tried to draw a family tree that would show who my ancestors were and how I thought all those people in our household were related. But I couldn't do it. I just didn't know how. What I ended up with wasn't a tree at all but a network of lines going every which way and showing relationships that I don't think would pass the test for what's considered normal.

I thought about blood tests. I thought about genetic testing. I saw those ads on television about looking into your ancestry and thought about finding out if it was true, as I had been told, that my ethnic origins were German, Irish, Native American, Italian, and Arabic!

I learned a few things. Mostly, I learned that I will probably never know for sure my relationship to anyone in the house I grew up in, including the man who first sexually abused me. A girl I thought was my cousin, who was adopted away from our family early on, may actually be my sister. And in fact, she and I have reconnected, first through Facebook and then in person, and we have resumed and really developed a relationship. Other bloodlines are so blurred that thinking about all the ways I may be related to this one or that one just blows my mind.

When I was a child I was told that my grandmother passed away before I was born. That was not true. I've now heard that my mother was adopted, so she herself might not know where she came from either. That means I really have no certainty who my biological parents are, but I would be grateful if someone could provide that certainty.

In the end, trying to find out the so-called facts of my so-called family didn't really answer any questions at all; instead, it just raised a lot of doubts. My head spins when I try to think about where I come from, who is truly my family, and how to put it all together. In one sense it makes my whole background look made up. In another, it doesn't mean a thing. Because I'm here, and I know who I am.

I'm not the sum of all the confusing information about my biological family. I am not defined by lines on a chart going down the generations. Which ancestor or ethnic group gave me my strength, my iron will, the backbone that enabled me to survive everything I've been through doesn't matter. What matters is that the strength was there when I needed it. The way I grew up hurt me, but it doesn't define me. I grew up in a pretty perverse atmosphere, but I live a normal, upright, respectable sort of life. The brutality that family members and Ariel Castro carried out against me didn't make me a brutal person. I strive every day to be kind to others, especially those who have suffered the kinds of abuse I know all too well.

I may have grown up with the wrong idea about the identities of the people in my "family." I may have been lied to. But I don't need to be defined by who I'm related to. I am my own person. I am the person who has proved herself stronger than a lifetime of violent and punishing abuse, both physical and emotional. I am a person with a caring heart and a concern for others in trouble or despair. I am the loving wife of a good and sweet man, and I am the birth mother of a fine boy I hope to meet again someday. The exact identities of some of the people who raised me can't ever take any of that away from me.

THIS DOES NOT mean that I don't want to confront my family in person. It is the main reason I might like to see some members of my family again. As I write this, I know that one of my aunts is not well. Although she was a part of my painful childhood, I do not wish anything bad for her; I hope she finds some kind of peace.

My mother is another story. At the time of my rescue in 2013 she took the opportunity to sound off about my childhood. She went on national television and "recalled" a childhood for me that in my mind never existed—a happy time when she and I were close and I fed the pony next door. There was no pony. And if my mother and I were ever close, it was because as any very young child would, I looked to her for love and protection. I felt I got neither.

What I see as her failure as a mother left me with long-lasting scars. It took a lot of healing from the inside to start learning to love myself, which I had to do before I could ever love somebody else. It took a long time and a lot of healing before I could let myself know that what I see in the mirror is not ugly; it is, as my husband tells me, beautiful.

I do not want to hurt my mother, but I want her to know how I feel about what happened to me as a child and that it mattered to me. Maybe my mother will read this book and come to understand how badly I feel I was hurt, and how the way I lived as a child left me with what I believe are permanent wounds, physical and emotional, and empty spaces in my heart and soul. I do not understand, and I'm not even going to try. I spent enough time trying as a child. I tried to get her attention. I tried to show her that I was an intelligent little girl with needs and hopes and fears, but I never felt like she realized this or paid me enough attention.

Yes, I am prepared to believe it was all because she was unhappy with her own life and took her frustrations out on me. But how could a mother act like that? I use the word "mother" loosely in her case because she never acted the way I thought a mother was supposed to act. It seemed like she never supported me or anything I did. She simply wasn't there as a mother.

Maybe reading these words will help her understand just how and how much she affected my life. Long ago I gave up trying to tell her anything because I felt that no matter how much I tried to tell her, she would just look at me like it wasn't happening. This was my reality; I need to acknowledge it. If my mother could ever understand how this reality affected me, I can imagine forgiving her. It is up to her. But I can never forget.

Shortly after I started writing this book, I learned that the man who first sexually abused me as a child had died. I did not shed a tear. I never will.

TODAY MY LIFE is blessed with a loving family around me. They are family according to the second definition of *family*, the kind of family defined as people who love you, care about you, keep you safe. In fact, I call these people my safe circle. You've met most of them: Anita and Erna, Jim, Kenny, Carol and Rose, a few more. I'll have more to say about them in Chapter 10, but trust me when I say that even without a blood tie between us, we're family. What connects me to each of them and each of them to me is stronger and thicker than blood ties any day. It's why I have a tattoo that says, "Family members don't have to be blood." They just have to be caring.

The life I live now is all about choices. I chose the family I have today, my safe circle, in the same way I chose to change my life around, the same way I chose a new name to start a new life. I chose to not be like my biological family. I chose to unlearn everything that was taught to me by what I saw around me when I was growing up. I chose instead to learn a new way to live and to be different from what my background might have determined I would become. I chose to be who I am.

CHAPTER NINE

A Life's Work, a Soul's Injury

I had to learn to give myself grace when I make mistakes—and to learn from them . . .

CHOOSING TO BE who I am is also how and why I chose my life's work.

I've never shied away from hard work. As I mentioned earlier, about the first thing I set out to do after my rescue was to get out there and get a job. For one thing, I needed to make a living, but I also wanted to focus on something outside myself that would bring me into contact with others and that might in some way make use of all I had been through and all I had learned. But everywhere I went looking for a job, I was told they couldn't hire me because I was a celebrity. The word struck me as pretty ironic. I certainly wasn't a celebrity in the way most people think of celebrity. It wasn't like I attended gala events and showed up on the red carpet and got asked what designer dress I was wearing. But I also have to admit that I understood what employers were saying. In any job where I would come in contact with the public, I would find myself being asked to appear in selfies or to sign autographs. Not a lot would get done.

In time, of course, I found work, nontraditional work, and I found it because people felt I had something important to say and to give.

Simply put, my life's work right now is to talk about subjects that, unfortunately, I know a lot about—namely, the kind of domestic violence and abuse, including sexual abuse, that goes on everywhere in the world. Through no fault of my own, I am an expert on these subjects, and if my expertise can help even a single person or change a single life for the better, that is all the fulfillment I need. I have a pretty full schedule of speaking engagements on these subjects, and I address all kinds of audiences: victims and survivors of violence and abuse, law enforcement officials, social services providers, doctors and nurses, people who run shelters, people who raise money, students and teachers. And as every reader of this book knows, I am also an author.

I have been making speeches and addressing these various audiences for several years now, yet I am nervous every time I get up and am about to begin speaking. The first time I ever got up in front of an audience to deliver a talk, I was so nervous that I didn't think any sound would come out if I opened my mouth. I had to figure a way to calm myself. I took a deep breath, and I said to myself: *Everything is going to be okay. It's going to be just like talking to a best friend, or to a Hostess Twinkie wearing overalls.* I don't know where that image came from, but it seemed to work. Even so, speaking in public to an audience was a struggle at first. What helped was that I knew what I had to tell them, I knew that my purpose was to give them strength and courage, and I just told it like I knew it.

Even today, however, the nervousness never really goes away. I do find that if I can interact with people in the audience a bit before we start, if I can hear some of their stories, that motivates me to really focus on their concerns and precisely target what I need to say.

I know it is against what the experts advise to say this, and my PR team will probably tear their hair out when they read this, but I never prepare a speech ahead of time. I never write out a script. For one thing, I am more at ease when I speak from the heart rather than reading something. But mostly I know in my bones and my skin what I want to say to these audiences. I know the points I want to make, depending on the subject matter and the audience.

If I am addressing women who face domestic violence from husbands or boyfriends, my message to them is: "Don't wait. If you wait, all you're doing is very likely just extending the time that you and your children are being hurt. Your abuser will continue to try to control you—that's what abusers do."

Kids are a tougher audience. I want to be able to reach them, but I also fear that telling them what I went through may be damaging for them to hear. My first instinct is their well-being, not mine, so I always check with the adults in charge of the talk about how far to go with any audience of children or teenagers or even older. Often many of the kids in the audience have already been damaged by abusers, and I have to choose what I say very carefully.

For those kids I remind them that you never know how strong you are until being strong is the only choice you have left. "When that happens," I say, "giving up is not an option. Keep hoping."

"There is life after darkness," I tell them, "and there are endless possibilities once you reach the light."

I also want these kids to keep in mind that, no matter what, they have control over who they are and what they will become. I tell a little bit of my own story, about people calling me "used goods" and saying no man would ever love or care for me, and that nobody would ever be a true friend to me. "Look at my life now," I tell them. "I am valued by a loving husband and safely surrounded by a circle of wonderful friends—all because *I* changed my life. No one changed it for me. No one else can."

"Yes, the scars are still there," I tell them, "and they won't go away, but now I look to the future."

I can only hope that the kids and teenagers I talk to hear what I'm saying and take it to heart. But they can be hard to reach.

The toughest audience I ever had, though—an audience I could never imagine as Hostess Twinkies in overalls—was a prison audience of men convicted of having abused women, in some cases, to death. Some of these men were in for life, but not all of them. And my initial thought was to try to reach the younger men, those who would eventually get out of prison, men whose assaults had not ended in murder.

I sat there and spilled my guts to these guys as I tried to relate what it is like to be one of their victims. I pulled no punches as I told them what their violent behavior feels like on the receiving end, what it does to the body, the soul, the sense of self. I told them how their violence kills even when it doesn't result in death. Half of them were weeping, the other half were praying in the back of the room as I went on. When I had finished, several of them said to me that my talk would change their lives and save them from ever committing violent assault again.

"Why did it take me to save you?" I asked. Why did it take a talk from a survivor of brutality to learn what brutality can do?

One of them answered for all. "Because we never really had somebody that actually sat down and had a conversation like this with us," he said. "We have only ever heard from people who judged us and labeled us for what we did in our past."

I hope that talk made a difference, but the responsibility and the ability to change still depends on each individual there. It was easy for them to *say* they were going to change, but words are lame unless real action follows, and I can only pray that my talk motivated action in at least some of them.

Someone once asked if I thought it might have made a difference if Ariel Castro had heard a talk like the one I gave that day. My answer was that I think he was too far gone. There are some people who are literally impossible to save. That's why I wanted to reach the young men in the group. Maybe it wasn't too late for them; maybe they were still able to change. I hope so.

I know that they too had suffered abuse. They too were damaged. But I reminded all the men that they still had a choice to get help to stop their pain; they could always choose a different route for dealing with their pain. Whatever had happened in their lives to make them violent criminals, they could choose to change their lives around. I know because I changed mine.

I KNOW that I will always be associated in some way with helping people avoid, escape, or be sheltered from abuse. When
I think about how I can do this full time in the future, I think
about starting a foundation through which I can found and
maintain a transition shelter.

Transition moments are crucial intersections in the lives
of women and children who suffer abuse. One of my models
for how to think about transitions is the Purple Project, an
Ohio-based organization that helps foster kids ease out of
the system and into society successfully. It organizes a range
of services that provide safety, teach life and work skills, and
even help the kids find formal wear for a prom or other
special occasions. I have been a speaker at Purple Project
events, and its founder and director, the remarkable Latasha
C. Watts, is a close friend and a member of my safe circle.

The combination of services Purple Project provides,
covering practical goals as well as the things that young people care about, is what I find so compelling. I think of Purple Project as a model for the transition center I hope to
call Lily's Ray of Hope, a women's shelter that I promise will
never turn anyone away. If there is no room at all, Lily's Ray
of Hope will find a place for the woman, and we will get her
there. No one will be sent away. Not ever.

That promise was born when I ran away from home the
Thanksgiving after my son, Joey, was born. It was very cold

out, but I was in such a hurry that I didn't even have time to get my coat. I put Joey in my shirt, and we walked and walked until I finally found us a shelter. But it had no room and could offer us no other options.

We kept going. Another two miles. Nobody stopped to help us. Nobody even looked at us. I had no money even to make a phone call to Carol and Rose, and their house was way too far away to walk to. The weather was scary. I kept talking to Joey, kept promising him that "eventually," we would arrive someplace. I was walking as fast as I could. I could hear him crying and I could tell he was very cold. I didn't want to steal, but I took a blanket off someone's porch and wrapped Joey in it as we walked. Several days later I returned that blanket.

I finally found a shelter—co-ed, with no privacy—that let us in for the night so long as we left first thing the next morning. I asked about transition assistance and was told, "You have to transition yourself." That about killed me. If I could transition myself, I probably wouldn't be walking coatless through the city looking for a bed for myself and my baby. Even today many shelters do not offer the kind of support services too many women and children need. They might refer you to some agency or other, but not everyone has money for a bus ride. Some are just too worn down to go another step.

Lily's Ray of Hope will offer all those options right on site: counseling, education, basic health care, privacy—because boundaries are important. I see the center as something like an apartment complex with studio-like apartments, each woman in her own room, all the women able to cook their meals.

It will offer safety and compassion, welcome and support. I want it to help women work toward their goals, not to do it for them. I want to create a place where women can have their own safe circles of other women who understand.

Another key model for Lily's Ray of Hope is One Safe Place, the California-based organization that I first discovered in the Cayman Islands. They do it right. So does AVDA, Aid to Victims of Domestic Abuse, in Florida, another great organization. I'd like to take the best of what these and other organizations do and bring it to Cleveland.

Lily's Ray of Hope will also, of course, offer art therapy classes in which women can express what they're going through in painting, drawing, writing, or music. As they do so, they may be able to learn to trust again.

But the transition center is not my only goal for the future. I would also love to create a paint-and-sip that would give people a creative outlet for fun and a kind of escape from the stress of their lives, whatever that stress might be. At Lily's Paint-and-Sip I would sometimes choose the paints and the subject. Other times the theme or assignment would be for people to paint whatever they want to paint. Classes for children would offer chips and healthy drinks. Classes for adults would offer snacks too, but only those adults who can prove they have a designated driver will be allowed alcohol.

For me, Lily's Ray of Hope and Lily's Paint-and-Sip are dreams for the future. But as you know by now, my dreams are always built with hope.

As YOU'VE been reading throughout this book so far, getting to the point where I can even think about a future has been a process. It didn't happen all at once. At first, in fact, I didn't really think about dealing with what I had been through. I didn't *want* to deal with it. I didn't want people to know about it, and I was certainly not prepared to open up to others. Partly I was afraid of what people might think of me, but mostly I guessed how much it would hurt to lay bare the wounds of my life. So in the beginning, after I was rescued from Castro's house, that was the last thing I wanted to do. I told myself that if the physical wounds healed, that would be enough.

But it wasn't.

IT WAS BACK in Chapter 5 that I told how, at the trauma center in Tennessee, I first opened up about my childhood and my captivity on a person-to-person basis. The audience back then was small, to say the least, and it was made up of total strangers I was unlikely to see again. Yes, I had then written my story in a book, had gone on a book tour and

talked to reporters and interviewers, had talked into micro-
phones or to audiences of people I couldn't see, and had
answered multiple questions, but all of that, important as
it was in lessening my pain, seemed anonymous to me. In a
way I might have been talking to the air. At the trauma center, however, I spoke face to face with other trauma victims,
people who could react and respond to what I was saying.
And they did—although, as it turns out, their response was
totally loving, like a warm embrace. But as I told you, I wasn't
comfortable even about doing that until I had been at the
center for a while, until I had been with those people for
a while and had gotten to know them somewhat. Even the
equine therapy with Waylon didn't especially inspire me to
talk openly to other people about what I had gone through
in my life. The value of Waylon was that whatever I said to
him was between the two of us. Talking to him was like looking at my feelings in a mirror. So it wasn't really until I heard
one after another of the other people at the trauma center
tell the stories of their own abuse that I felt I could tell mine.
I understood what they had suffered because I recognized it,
and I realized that they would understand my pain for the
same reason: because they recognized it. They knew where I
was coming from and what I had been through because they
had been there as well. They wouldn't judge me.

It was a huge help to me to see how much being able
to open up the wounds of what I suffered in Castro's house
actually helped my healing process. But it took another four
years, until 2017, before I was able to open up a wound that

went way back in my life. The wound I opened up to others then, the wound I am opening up to all my readers here and now, is my soul injury.

There is actually a program called Soul Injury. It was started by a nurse and a bereavement counselor who had worked for a long time caring for military veterans, especially vets at the end of their lives. The two found that a great many of these veterans waited until just before death to finally reveal "what damaged their soul." It kind of burst out of them on their deathbeds, and it was only then, and only by revealing these injuries, that the dying veterans were able to release the hold the injuries had on their lives.

It makes sense. A lot of veterans who have experienced some form of trauma try hard to put a lid on it when they get home from the war. Keeping the lid on tightly can work while they are in the prime of life, but as they near death, the unconscious mind grows stronger, and the memories won't stay pushed down. The memories sort of explode out of these onetime soldiers, but by then it's pretty late, and as for the peace the veteran may gain as a result, it's really too late to enjoy its benefits. The founders of Soul Injury saw that waiting until just before death to break the hold of such wounds meant that these vets spent most of their adult lives in pain and unable to become all they could be or achieve all they wanted to achieve. The ongoing impact of their soul injury limited their lives. So the two founded the Soul Injury program to help turn that around.

But the two founders also understood that you didn't need to have been in the military to experience a soul injury. Any kind of trauma can cause it. People who have suffered abuse or lost their health or lived in a war zone or survived a terrible disaster—not to mention the people who care for traumatized people—can all suffer damage to their souls.

The founders of the Soul Injury organization define a soul injury as a pain that "can subtly and not-so-subtly rob traumatized people of their vitality. The source of soul injury is unmourned grief and unforgiven guilt and shame over things we think we should or should not have done. Unmourned grief and unforgiven guilt can sabotage lives."* They do that by making the person feel tainted in some way—stained. Because there was no support or protection at the time of the original injury, the person feels totally disrupted and disconnected and not worth much of anything, and that becomes like a mark on that person. A blemish. Something that doesn't rub off easily.

I know exactly what they mean. I know from very personal experience what unmourned grief and unforgiven guilt are all about, and I know how they sabotaged my life. Guilty and ashamed and disconnected and worthless—I'm familiar with those feelings . . . and with the fear they can put into you and the stain they can leave on you. By 2017 I

---

*"Healing the Deepest Pain," Soul Injury, February 15, 2015, www.soul injury.org/healing-the-deepest-pain.

realized that if I was to live life at all, I had to reveal what had damaged my soul and begin to deal with it—the sooner the better. If I kept on waiting, I might carry the weight of it all my life, and I did not want that. I did not want to be on my deathbed before I healed my soul injury. I had to heal it now.

I received an invitation to be a keynote speaker for a Soul Injury program in the spring of 2017. I should say co-keynote speaker: I was paired with an Army veteran who had also been asked to share his story. We had been booked for two days, a Monday and a Tuesday in early June, to reach two different audiences. The events were held in funeral parlors in two towns not very far from Cleveland. Why in funeral parlors? Because a lot of funeral homes around the country are involved in Soul Injury outreach efforts to reach people who deal with grief and bereavement in their work—like the audiences I was invited to talk to.

I remember that the day before, Sunday, had been really hot—more like summer than spring for Cleveland—but Monday was a nice spring day, and I was feeling pretty good as Miguel drove me to Strongsville for the first day's meeting.

The meeting was held in a great big room in the funeral home. Chandeliers and recessed lighting made it a bright place, and a patterned green-and-gold carpet covered the floor and made the room feel quiet and serene—just right for a funeral parlor, I thought. As the room kept filling up, more chairs were brought in, and by the time the program was ready to begin, there were so many people that they had run out of chairs and some people were standing against the walls. I had been told that the audience would consist of nurses, doctors, caseworkers, veterans, cops, therapists, and even the family members of some victims of trauma—all people who had some experience, direct or indirect, with soul injury.

First, there was a video meant to set the context of the program. It featured individuals who had held onto a re-membered trauma very deeply and for a very long time until finally something in their heads clicked, and they were ready to open the wound. All of them said how much speaking aloud their soul injury had helped them. That sounded right to me. A soul injury makes dealing with life difficult, and beginning to heal the injury can immediately help put you back in life.

Maybe it was during the video or when the organizer of the event introduced my co-speaker and me and said we were there to tell our soul injuries, but at some point I got it into my head to mention my son. As you know, I don't script my speeches ahead of time, and I really had no clear idea what I would be saying when my turn came. I just knew something would pop into my head. I had often mentioned Joey during speaking engagements—always very briefly, just a mention, and I figured that whatever I ended up talking about to this group, I could also mention Joey in my speech.

By now, however, I was eager to hear the veteran's story of his soul injury, so I asked him to go first. He talked about Army training and then being sent overseas on active duty with his group—I don't know to which area of conflict; I'm not sure he named a place, and I'm not sure it matters. He told about how he and the guys in his group all bonded very tightly—they were a band of brothers. Then one day they went out on patrol and came under attack, and every single member of the group was killed—except him. Helplessly he watched one after the other of his band of brothers die. But he did not die. He was alive, and that became guilt and shame and terrible inner pain for him.

As he spoke, the audience responded openly. Nobody held back. People cried. People yelled encouragement. When he talked about the very valuable therapy he had undergone—not my experience, as you know—people listened attentively. I was reminded then that many in the audience were themselves therapists and caregivers.

I was riveted to his story, and as it unfolded, something clicked in my head: *Here and now,* I thought. *This meeting today would be the right setting and the right moment to really tell my soul injury.* I think I knew at that moment that I didn't have to be afraid or ashamed to reveal what I had tried so hard to bury as deeply as possible so very long ago. And I felt that if I did, I might finally bring into the light something that I still had kept in the dark.

The vet finished, and it was my turn. I stood up. And I began by admitting that although I often mentioned my son in talks I gave, I had never really told anyone before what I was about to tell them—and am now about to tell you. I had not written about it in *Finding Me.* I had not talked about it at the trauma center. I had not even fully shared it with

Miguel. "The wound I'm going to open up," I said, "is my soul injury." I was quite nervous when I began to talk; the butterflies in my stomach were so bad that I felt a little like I might be sick, and I actually had to swallow it back a couple of times. I started again, and it was so difficult that, at first, the organizer had to help me along. I was talking about being unable to control my own life, and I was losing my own self-control as I was telling about it. I had to stop at certain points. But as I kept going I could sense that the people in the audience understood exactly what I was talking about. They saw exactly how I was hurting. I cried almost the whole way through my story, but as I kept going, I felt a weight beginning to lift. I felt a certain sense of relief.

After a while the story just poured out of me. Here is what I told the Soul Injury audience:

Very early on, I chose a bad road for my life. I can say that I chose this road because it was all I knew. I learned it—I learned everything—from people who were not healthy for my life, who were poisoning my life. I learned from being sexually abused. From being beaten by family members. From being told I was nothing. When you get told you're nothing over and over and over, you start believing it.

But still, I am the one who made the choice. I am the one who followed a path down the bad road. I started drinking booze when I was ten years old. I started doing drugs when I was eleven. I did both as a way to suppress everything I was going through in my life. To numb my feelings.

I still kept trying to tell people what was going on in my life. I tried to get grownups—people in authority—to listen and understand. Nobody did. They told me I was lying. They accepted it when my mother and other family members denied what I was saying, when my mother would say, "I'm a good parent. I didn't do anything wrong."

But I felt that my family did do something wrong, and because I couldn't stop it, I allowed them to hurt me to the point where I hurt myself. Three times I almost committed suicide. Each time I got close but couldn't go through with it.

I was not yet eighteen years old when I found out I was pregnant. That was a turning point for me. If nobody was going to do anything to help me, I was going to have to do it myself. I knew there was a better way to live, and now that I had another life growing inside me, this seemed the time to try. So I locked myself in a room and determined that I was going to detox myself—get rid of all the alcohol and drugs I had been taking in. Get clean and sober.

This is how I would be different from my family. I would get off the bad road I was on, and I would break with my family and everything about them. I wanted my baby to have a better life. What I did not realize was that what I was deciding to do could actually hurt him.

I told myself that everything would be okay. I had a supply of bread and lots of water and I told myself, *I'm going to do this and I'm going to fight for my child and nothing bad can happen. Nothing is going to stop me from doing this.* Hurting the baby beginning to grow inside me or hurting myself was the furthest thing from my mind. But after two weeks of being in the room by myself, I was severely dehydrated. I was also weak from lack of food because everything that I ate I threw up. I had hot and cold flashes. My body was numb. I could barely walk. I had to more or less drag myself to a phone to call the doctor.

I said to the doctor, "I feel like I'm dying right now, and I am pregnant, so I am coming to the hospital!"

Honestly, I don't remember how I got there, but when I did, the medical staff told me that if I had waited any longer, I could have lost both the baby and myself. They fixed me up, and then they sent me home, ordered me to rest, said I would need to drink plenty of water and eat plenty of food and take some vitamins to make sure the baby stayed healthy. They assured me it was all right, that the baby was "just a little seed" and would grow healthier over time.

But "home" didn't provide the rest or the healthy food I needed. I was still being abused, still being beaten, still being told I was nothing. At twenty-four weeks I started bleeding and went to the hospital again. The first thing they asked me was if I was okay. "No," I said. I was kind of frantic. I told them I was afraid that I had hurt myself and my little unborn child so much that I felt like I was going to lose him. I told them I was still being abused and hurt in terrible ways at home. I wanted them to know that, but from long experience I knew no one was listening.

They just focused on the pregnancy. The medical staff told me that everything could be okay, that this was just a minor setback. "As long as you stay very comfortable," they told me, "the pregnancy will be all right." I think I spent a week in the hospital—at the time everything was pretty much a blur.

When I was released from the hospital they told me I should not climb stairs. But my bedroom was upstairs, and my family members—my mother, my uncle—had no interest in moving the rooms around. As usual, they didn't want to do anything for me, so I had to do everything myself. I went upstairs and carried my mattress and my bed downstairs. Once again I thought how I was hurting myself to make my family comfortable, doing everything they wanted me to do instead of them doing something—anything—to help me.

It wasn't long before I went back to the hospital, this time with cramping and a headache. My "uncle" was with me. "Are you drinking plenty of water?" I was asked. "Have you been climbing stairs? Exerting yourself physically?" He was sitting right there—my abuser. I couldn't answer truthfully. I couldn't say, "If I tell you the truth, I'll get beaten when I get home." I just told them I hurt. I hurt. I hurt.

Shortly after that, I started leaking amniotic fluid. I went to the hospital again, and again my uncle took me. This time I was told I needed complete pelvic rest and bed rest. The doctor, a man, said to me, "You've got to stop having sex."

"Sure," I said, "you tell the person that's doing it to me."

"What are you talking about?" the doctor asked me.

I told him. I said I was being forced to have sex, that in no way was it my choice.

He asked who was forcing me and how it was happening, and I thought back on all the times I had tried to tell "responsible adults" what was happening and said to him, "If I tell you, you're not going to help me anyway."

He walked out of the room and sent in a woman doctor, and I told her exactly the same thing: "For years I've been trying to tell you people that I've been abused. You shoved me away. You told me I was lying. You told me it wasn't possible. Now I'm here again. I'm trying to tell you again without saying it. The person who is forcing me is sitting right over there, and you still haven't done anything about it."

You know what? Once again nothing happened. The hospital sent me home. I went home with my abuser. And as soon as we got through the door I was beaten again—for telling tales out of school, for talking about "the family" in front of others. As always, I was stuck. If I ran to Carol and Rose, some family member would just come and get me. And I had no source of income for myself. Any money I ever got—even for babysitting when I was a kid—they took from me.

I stayed. I felt I had no choice. I had broken with my family, had tried to escape the life I was born into, and I had lost. I felt everything a soul-injured person feels: shame, guilt, a loss of any sense of self, pain, heartache, hopelessness.

As I brought my story to a close, I could see and hear people in the audience crying. So I finished by telling them about the birth of my son. I wanted them to know that something very, very good—my son—had come out of all this. I told them about how I had to have a Caesarean section and that Joey emerged unresponsive. I told them about watching the nurses and doctor take my baby away, over to the side of the room, and about the tears of joy that came streaming down my face when I heard him scream. I was so happy he was alive! But I also let them know that others had raised my son.

"To this day," I told the Soul Injury audience, "I feel grief because I never told anybody what I have just told you. I never said anything. I never wanted people to know because I was afraid of what they would think. Only today do I realize that I'm tired of what everybody else thinks and I need to get this off my chest before it hurts me any more than it already has."

I sat down. The audience applauded.

It felt so good to have told about this injury. It felt good to have spoken this truth. I know that revealing it strengthened me, makes me more comfortable in my own skin and, I believe, more effective as an advocate for others with soul injuries, whoever they are and whatever their age. Do I wish I had done it before? There's a right time for these things. Everybody heals in their own way. I had to wait until I was ready. The time and place were part of it. The veteran's bravery in telling his story was inspirational. Everything came together. My heart, soul, and mind connected, and I could bring this story out of the darkness into the light.

The next day Miguel drove me to Parma, Ohio, where I told the story all over again to another Soul Injury audience. The weight of guilt and shame got even lighter.

CHAPTER TEN

Safe Circle

I don't take a single thing for granted . . .

I'M THE EARLY RISER in the family. Miguel likes to stay up much later at night than I do, so he sleeps later in the morning too. For me, after eleven years of living on a daily schedule totally determined by Castro's insanity, I still haven't completely adjusted back to anything normal. It's still hard for me to eat three meals a day at the standard times most people eat breakfast, lunch, and dinner. And I still wake up at funny times of night or early morning.

Sometimes I'm awakened by animal sounds, which of course is fine with me—I love waking up to animal noises. We hear all different types of animals out where we live, which is farther away from the city than my first house. Where we are now feels like real country, especially with the big trees we have in the backyard, and we hear animals I never got to hear when I was growing up. We hear foxes. We hear coyotes. There are two different types of owls, but I am not sure what their names are because I haven't yet spotted them. But they start up at about two or three in the morning, and one goes *Hoo Hoo,* and the other goes *Hmmm Hmmm.* One of them lives in my tree, but I still have never been able to see him.

I keep trying though. Every morning I take my mug of coffee out back onto the deck and just listen to the owls. I watch the other birds, and I watch the squirrels going about their business in their highly organized way, and I watch the trees bend in the wind.

I go out there in every weather. As I've said before, after eleven years in hell that I thought would never end, mornings in my own backyard with a cup of coffee and the beauty of nature are a precious blessing for me, and I like to breathe in every second of it, whether I'm wrapped in a blanket or just in my bathing suit.

This is how I choose to start just about every day—quietly and peacefully. It's one reason I try to schedule appointments or speaking engagements later in the day. I tell people I'm not "a morning person," and as far as meetings and appointments are concerned, I'm not. But mostly mornings are the time I reserve to myself. That's when I get my head in order, get myself geared up, take the time to taste my life as it is now—life after darkness.

Mine is really a pretty simple life. Sometimes on weekdays I might be traveling and my sweetie might be on the job, but when we're both here at home, like on a weekend, we're really here. Today was like that. I let Miguel sleep and mostly just dawdled around outside for a while. I played with the dogs and ran them around the yard a couple of times—the running is good for them, providing them an early-morning workout that takes a lot of energy, which helps them stay a little bit calm when I bring them back inside. On winter mornings, when it may just be too cold to stay outdoors for long, I mostly just hang out in the kitchen and maybe listen to some music. Then, when I figure it's time, I'll go into the bedroom and wake up Miguel. Gently.

This morning I woke him by giving him a kiss on his cheek. He got right awake. "What's up?" he said. "What are we doing today?" I sat there on the edge of the bed, and we talked about the possibilities. We considered maybe going to the park, and we also thought about just staying home and chilling, maybe watching some movies. He asked about my upcoming travel schedule. I mentioned something about my plants in the backyard. Miguel isn't much into plants, but he knows I am, so he listened to what I had to say. The conversation moved on to our many animals.

"We really need to do something about that lizard that's growing too big," Miguel reminded me. We got some misinformation about the species when we bought the lizard, and it's about to outgrow the containment device we have for it—"and maybe turn into a dragon," I add. So we need to find the right kind of home for this animal, one that can deal with its size and eating habits.

Then we talked a little bit about where we are in each of our lives right at this moment and about our life together, and we decided we were "in a good place" both ways.

Once we were both up and dressed, we started doing odds and ends around the house together—little repairs and some house cleaning. If it were spring or summer, we would probably go out into the garden and get some gardening work done.

And then in the afternoon we each took some time in our separate spaces too. Miguel and a pal dove into his man cave, and I went into my feng shui room. In the man cave are a TV and two La-Z-Boy chairs, and I could hear the two of them yelling out loud as they watched sports on television. There's also a seventy-five-gallon fish tank in the man cave, and of course all of my sweetie's *Star Wars* stuff.

My feng shui room is where I have created what is, for me, the perfect environment where I can feel at home by myself and also be in harmony with nature right in my own house. The room has spacious windows that let in lots of light and air, when wanted. On the walls, which are painted a color called passion purple, are paintings and posters I have made plus photographs from the time of my rescue, my wedding pictures, and pictures of all my animals. A lot of the animals live in the room. The lizards are in a zoo containment cage, although when I'm in the room I usually let them out so they can race around freely. The guinea pigs are in a huge cage that I keep on top of the bookcase because, if it were any lower, the dogs would bother the guinea pigs like crazy. And there's an aquarium, equipped with a waterfall, for the fish.

There's a daybed there for me to lie down on, a television, a sound system, and a storage container holding all my art supplies. When I'm not using them I pack them up in the storage box and keep the box in the corner.

Today I was using them a lot, working on a new painting. I do practically all my painting, my drawing, and my writing here—all the creative things that have been saving my life since I was a kid. Back then—and certainly when I was in Castro's house—I really had to scrounge for the tools and supplies to do these things. I had to be as creative about what I could use as a tool as I was about the drawing or writing itself, and one of the joys of my life today is that I have all the tools and supplies I need. Today I have art equipment

I never even imagined existed: different stencils that help me make straight shapes, others that help me make curved shapes, different brushes and even metal objects to paint with, acrylic paint with paint thinner so I can flip the brush and make a pretty little pattern on what I've just painted. I use that to make it look like there are actually leaves growing on the trees. Then I have this little palette knife that doesn't cut the palette board—unless you go too deep. I can spend hours at my art, surrounded by my animals, in my feng shui room. In fact, that's exactly how I spent today.

Then, in the evening, my sweetie made dinner. Unless we're out at a restaurant with some friends from our safe circle, one or the other of us is the chef, depending on what we're in the mood for. We each have our own different areas of cooking expertise. He is the grilling expert, and I am the sandwich expert. Tonight it was burgers on the grill, and then we settled down in front of the television in the living room and chilled. Miguel, of course, found the comedy shows he likes on TV, and we laughed until our lips felt numb.

He was still laughing when I got up and went to bed, earlier than him, as usual, while he stayed up to watch late-night TV.

This is such a good life, and as I think any reader of this book can appreciate, I cherish every moment of it. I am aware, just about every moment I'm alive, of what I have gained, what I have learned, and how far I have come in these five years since I was rescued.

It is all summed up for me in the fact that I am able to reach people through the talks I give and through my advocacy work, and when I come home from the work, there is my sweetie. There are the dogs and the lizards and the turtles, the trees and the plants, our wonderful house—and each other.

Not that our life is all peaches and cream. Of course it isn't. Like most couples, we disagree sometimes, and we each have our frustrations. The life we're living—caught in the public eye—is new to both of us, and we're finding our way. It is one reason we each have our separate spaces in the house—his man cave and my feng shui room—so we can get some space when we need to. Miguel made some major adjustments in his life so I could keep on doing the speaking engagements and meetings that have become my life's work. That has not always been easy for him. But we both feel protective of each other and of our time together. I'll let him tell the story his way:

> I'm a forty-hour-a-week, everyday kind of Joe, have been since I was a teenager, so all of this is new to me. It's just not in my nature not to work steadily at a particular job, so yes, I've had to adjust. Living with a public figure puts me out there a little, and

it can be rough. She has qualities of strength I just don't have, but then she sees qualities in me that she doesn't have. And actually, she has brought out better qualities in me that I didn't know I had. So we fit well.

I never thought I would ever get married, but she is different from everyone else I've ever encountered in my life. She comes with her past, and she comes with her strength of character, which is amazing. How she still is the person she is after all she's been through— so positive—I still don't understand. Where does it come from? Anyone who gets an opportunity to know her is amazed by her.

Because of her eyesight, she can't drive, so when she needs to get around for most local appointments, I'm her legs. I worry about her all the time when I'm not with her. All the time. Even though I know she knows how to take care of herself better than anybody, when she's out there, anything can happen. There is a whole strange universe out there. Anything can happen.

I also worry about the things she has to deal with. All the business details. Contracts can be nerve-wracking—they're in another language. And there are things that can't be settled right away. We need to put them off to the side to wait for a response or for somebody else. That's frustrating too.

Mostly it's playing a public role that's tough. It affects how we feel day by day. But this is the card we've been dealt, so it's the card we play. It is what it is.

I feel protective. You know, she has a hundred thousand followers on her Facebook page, and most of them are great. Some are critical, but I don't mind the criticism she gets at all. I really don't care what anyone says, because they don't know anything about her, and they don't know the truth of our life. I think people are more entertaining themselves when they write those kinds of posts. What I do worry about are the ugly posts. People writing things like "You don't deserve your good life" or "You had it all handed to you." That stuff bothers me. Lily got nothing handed to her. Neither did I. We worked for everything we have. We did it ourselves.

Sometimes the ugly posts get threatening. "I hope you die a horrible death." Who writes such things?

We get a lot of shallow comments too. People we sort of know who might think we're rich and look at our used car that looks brand new and say, "Wow, it must be nice."

"Think it's nice?" I answer them. "You can have the payments too."

Then there are the people who know somebody who knows somebody who knows me who tells Lily, "He's just with you for the money." I can't figure out why someone would say that, except that maybe they can't stand their own life.

We deal with all sorts of different things in our life. People come in and out of our lives. Some think they can take advantage of her kindness, and they vanish when they see that won't happen. Some do things that turn us off, and we just don't deal with them anymore. But her being a public figure can put a certain amount of stress on us any given day. It's hard to feel settled—settled *down*. We always kind of feel like our lives are on fast forward. Even on our honeymoon in Hawaii we sort of felt we had to keep moving. I know it will settle down in time. We're dealing with it, but while we wait, it's frustrating.

Yes, we have disagreements. We both get angry. But we try not to fight. We try to look for a solution. If nobody gets to win, sometimes we both have to lose. But at least we figure out a way so that we're not at each other's throats.

The dogs are an issue. I love the dogs, and I understand her passion for animals. But with everything else that is going on in our lives, four dogs seem to me to be too many, and sometimes it is overwhelming. I work at doing something out there in the backyard, and half the time the dogs wreck it and I need to go out and correct it all over again. But I know she can't give up the dogs, and I don't want her to feel something is being taken away from her. So we figure out a way to control the dogs a little, at least to keep them from interrupting everything.

She is such a great person—so deserving of a good life and real happiness. I never have been through any ordeal in my life, and I just can't believe her strength. This past year, when she has been finding out so much more about the lies that members of her family told her, has been an emotional roller coaster for her—and for me. It's like learning your whole life was a lie. Like: *Who are you really?* So she feels now in a way like what she thought she knew about her life has been overruled.

But she knows who she is. She is not her family. She is not her past. She is the positive, loving woman I see every day.

You can easily see why I love him so much. This is how we feel about each other every single day. We build each other up when our spirits get low. We know we have each other's backs, and we can take criticism with a grain of salt, even if it hurts. We both know that life is too short to let what people say affect how we live. A smile that passes between us, a gentle hug, a kiss—and our frustrations melt away. When we can't put into words how we feel, we say to each other, "Honey, take a breath. Let the words just roll off your tongue." When we disagree, we practice patience with each other. We find understanding and compromise. Is it easy? Not always. But we find a way to make it work. I wouldn't change that for the world. He is my other half.

We have the same mind. When our first anniversary rolled around, we gave each other anniversary gifts. From him to me: a silver picture frame. From me to him: A throw blanket. But both items were imprinted with the exact same image: a tree sprouting hundreds of hearts as leaves, with a pair of lovebirds on one of the branches. It's like the same idea inspiring us both.

Our friend Jasmine calls us the "sick-making couple." She says, "You two are so in love, it makes me sick!"

Of course, Jasmine is one of the friends in my safe circle. "Safe" means I don't worry they would ever try to "use" our friendship for their advantage. "Safe" means they would never hurt me. "Safe" means I can say whatever I feel like saying and laugh at whatever I think is funny when they're around, and it's never going to be posted on Facebook or show up on the news or in a book somewhere.

Some of the people in my safe circle are folks I met in that first year or so after coming out of Castro's house, folks who seemed to want to be around me because they cared. Anita, Erna, Jim, Kenny: When they asked how I was, it was because they really wanted to know. And when they said let's get together, it was because they genuinely valued spending time with me. They weren't out for anything. Unlike so many of the "new" friends I told you about earlier, they didn't see any advantage or profit in being with me. They just cared.

It took a while, but I finally realized that the people in my safe circle are the family I never had but always wanted. I believe, as totally as I believe anything, that they are here to help me when I fall, catch me when I trip, help me see when I'm blind. They're there for me.

And as I believe they know, I will always be there for them.

There are about a dozen people in this safe circle. You've met a lot of them. Anita is Mom and Erna is Grandma, the two women with longish blonde hair, big sunglasses, and all you have to do is see them smile to know you're home. Jim is Dad, the guy who walked me down the aisle at my wedding and gave me away to Miguel, the father everyone should wish for. Kenny is the silly uncle who cracks everybody up, and his girlfriend, Tracye, is the cool aunt you secretly like best of all the aunts you have. Kenny and Tracye are also the travelers in the group; they're always going off somewhere interesting and sending back photos that make us all jealous. Jeannette and Tim, Jackie, Jimmy, Jasmine, Rose and Joe, Carole, Latasha of Project Purple, of course.

Do we ever all get together as a group? Unfortunately, not easily and not often. I've found that trying to make a date for even four friends to get together and have dinner out takes more texts or emails than I can count. *Can we make it later because I have something going on at work? Can we make it earlier because I want to get home in time to see the game? Can we make it Tuesday instead of Wednesday or Monday instead of Thursday?* You're probably familiar with the same thing. If it takes that many emails and that much time to arrange a date for four, just think about trying to get more than *ten* people together at one time in one place. It is very tough to do. We try, though, especially for birthdays.

We like the kind of fun that depends on being together, not on drinking until you're blind, the way a few of us used to do. Instead, we enjoy going out to restaurants, comedy clubs, and, of course, karaoke clubs, but what we mostly like is getting together at our house. Especially in the warm weather, these friends are glad to come and hang out in our backyard. They love what Miguel has done with the yard—the pond and the waterfall, the stone walls, the plantings. "Hey, Lily," they'll kid with me, "can you give us Miguel so he can do the same thing with our backyards?" I joke right back, "You can borrow him, but you can't have him. He's mine."

When we're together the friends in my safe circle and I talk about our lives, our plans, what we're thinking and feeling. Just to be with them makes me feel completely protected and secure—and very happy. These people came into my life at a difficult time. They adopted me. They like me for who I am and care about me as a person—not because or in spite of what I went through in my past. They and my husband have showed me everything I had been missing in life all along—until they became my family.

CHAPTER ELEVEN

The Missing Child

I stand up in a crowd screaming in the middle of the room, and it feels like a thousand knives hit me all at once. Do you realize I am here? Do you see me? . . .

I HAVE SIXTY-THREE TATTOOS. So far, anyway.

People ask about them. *Why so many? Are they an attempt to reclaim your body after a lifetime of abuse?* No. Absolutely not. Rather, they are a visual exploration of my identity. They make up a canvas that holds the art and symbols and words that mean something to me. My tattoos chart the journey of who I've been, who I am, and who I'm becoming.

I was thirteen when I got my first tattoo. It was a very funny little smiley face that I thought at first was the sun smiling, but it was really just a dumb smiley face. It didn't mean anything to me, so later I covered it up with other tattoos.

The first tattoo I got after I was rescued is of a baby sleeping in a pair of hands. That was the first baby Castro forced me to miscarry. He even made me look at the fetus, which was tiny and barely developed at all. That's why I wanted the tattoo image to be faint, like it's fading from view. The baby also has a pair of wings. It's my angel being cradled in God's hands, and it's on my upper arm, where everyone can see it.

Around the sleeping baby are four roses. They represent the other four babies Castro made me abort. He starved me, beat me, threw me down the stairs—whatever it took to get rid of the babies.

Another tattoo comes from a drawing I made when I was still a captive. It's a teddy bear with a rose for a heart. I drew it for Joey one Valentine's Day, and as I drew it I made a promise to myself that when I got out of that house I was going to get that drawing tattooed onto me. I just knew I needed to have my son imprinted onto my skin. There's another Joey tattoo on my back: a cross with wings and his name. I don't see it, just like I don't get to see my son—at least not yet—but he's always with me. He is part of me and I am part of him.

Joey and the five babies I lost are my missing children. So is the child Miguel and I may never be able to have because of what Castro did to me. And there is one more missing child: me. I was a missing child twice over. First, I was lost in an unloving family and in a system that did not pay attention. Then I was kidnapped and presumed to be a runaway, so no one came looking for me.

THE WORDS under the title at the beginning of this chapter are something I once wrote about what it feels like to be a missing child. It is why I feel I can never stop speaking out on behalf of missing children—kidnapped, abused, in danger, lost. No one has a better right and no one knows more about the issue than those of us who have actually been through the experience. Putting my voice to work for missing children and for all victims of domestic violence—and extending a hand to the people searching for them—is the best way I can give meaning to my own suffering.

Put it this way: I should have died in that house. What that man did to me was enough to kill me a few times over. There must be a reason why God kept me alive, and it has got to be what I'm doing now: bringing awareness about missing and exploited children and about domestic violence, and giving hope to the mothers and fathers who have lost their children, encouraging them to keep pushing. I feel like this is the reason I was put back on this earth.

Obviously, the job's still not done.

I DON'T KNOW how many missing children there are. I know there's a website* that keeps a running total. As I write this, they're reporting nearly half a million missing children in America in 2016. Then there are the missing children no one may be counting, and then there is the rest of the world. Just thinking about what the real numbers might be blows my mind.

I also don't know how many of those kids or any other kids are being sexually abused, but I know the government's statistics[†] say that more than 42 percent of female rape victims were first raped before the age of eighteen, nearly 30 percent between the ages of eleven and seventeen, and that more than 12 percent of female rape victims and nearly 28 percent of male rape victims were first raped when they were ten years old or younger.

---

*National Center for Missing and Exploited Children, www.missingkids.com.

[†]"Sexual Violence Facts at a Glance," Centers for Disease Control, www.cdc.gov/violenceprevention/pdf/sv-datasheet-a.pdf.

Anybody can find any of these statistics on the internet any time.

What I do know is what it's like to be a little kid inside those statistics, and if I can raise my voice on behalf of them, I'll do it until I drop.

Then there are the women at the receiving end of domestic violence by a partner or spouse. Every nine seconds in America a man beats or assaults a woman he is living with or in a "relationship" with.* I know a thing or two about that kind of control and those kinds of beatings too, and I need to speak up about that as well.

Here's something else I know: when I ask audiences I'm addressing to close their eyes and then to raise a hand if they've ever been abused or know somebody who has been abused, the number of arms up is always higher than you would suspect. Always. In fact, anytime you find yourself in a crowded room—a movie theater, a stadium, a crowd at the airport—there is likely a woman or man standing near you who was abused as a child or is being abused right now. And that person has probably neither looked for nor found the help they need and deserve.

_____

*"Statistics," National Coalition Against Domestic Violence, https://ncadv.org/statistics.

MAYBE THE most important thing people need to know about what happened to me and is happening to children and women everywhere right now is that it can happen to anybody. It doesn't matter who you are—whether you're rich or poor, short, tall, fat, skinny, awkward, graceful, or anything else.

Take the case of my kidnapping. It was what they call "opportunistic": it wasn't planned, and it wasn't personal. Men like Castro don't care who they take; they don't think it out. They wait, they see you as a sexual object, you're within range of their power, and they want control because they feel they don't control anything else in their lives. A woman chained up or a little boy locked in a closet can't walk out the door. That's what guys like Castro want: for you to have no choice whatsoever, to be totally dependent on them. You're not a person; you're a thing they make use of. They rule.

Sometimes people can even victimize you without the chains and locked doors and boarded-up windows. They do it through bullying and talking down to you and making you feel insecure, unimportant, or invisible. People like that control you because they have torn you down so low that you're just broken. You're not going to try to escape or do anything "wrong" because you know what will happen if you do. And fear of what would happen if you walked out that door can sometimes be just as powerful a brake as being chained or locked up.

When I talk to groups about these subjects, people always come up to me afterward and say they're glad I made it out alive. Because I escaped, I now feel an obligation to keep speaking up about it. I wish I had known when it was happening to me that someone was out there saying something about it. So when I make my voice heard, I am doing it for the person suffering what I suffered and wishing that same wish.

This doesn't mean that it is easy for me to make speeches or be on panels or address even small groups. And it doesn't get any easier with time. For one thing, it is painful to share what I experienced, but making myself do it has become a key part of my healing process. Remember that I was raised to put my feelings aside, hold my tears in, and bite my tongue. So now I give myself grace to shed light and teach others what I know from having experienced abuse in more ways than I can count: emotionally, physically, sexually, verbally, and by being held captive.

To get through it, I imagine the people who might be listening, and I think about what my words might mean to them. I visualize a woman being bullied by her partner who hears me and begins to look at her life differently and finds the strength to make a change. I see in my head a young girl who thinks her life is worthless because people have told her she is ugly, too fat, too skinny. I hope she hears me and realizes that someone else knows what she's going through and understands—and maybe she will turn around and say, *I love myself for who I am and nothing that you can do can turn my smile upside down.* I think about the people who still need to come home as I did, and I think about the people still waiting for them to come home.

I warn kids about predators who may wait outside the school or playground. I tell them to yell "Fire!" or fight against or even bite someone if they have to in order to get people's attention. Don't worry about feeling silly: feeling silly can keep you safe.

And if nobody hears you and you are hurt, don't be afraid to tell someone about it. It was not your fault! So tell somebody you do trust. Don't wait. Hiding the pain only protects the person who hurt you and lets that person hurt others.

I often talk about body image and the criticism that some young people are sometimes cruel enough to deliver. I want all kids—but especially teenagers—to know that there isn't just one standard of beauty in the world. There isn't just one way to look, any more than there is just one way to think or one way to act.

If others criticize you or, worse, bully you, that is no reason to try to be what others think you should be. Most of the awful stuff people say to hurt your feelings is the stuff those people dislike about themselves. I recite some of the hurtful things I heard as a kid—that I was too short, that I had a big nose I should get fixed, that I looked like a clown, that I was too fat, and what was I thinking when I wore that outfit! I tell people I know how that hurts, but why on earth should all of us look the same? Why should we all try to look like those images we see everywhere? How boring and bland the world would be if we all looked the same. Instead, I think we should celebrate all the different beauties there are, remembering that true beauty is more than skin deep, and if you love yourself, you should love the unique way you were created and pay no attention to what other people say. As long as you love yourself, I tell teenagers, what others say doesn't matter. As long as you love yourself, you are beautiful. You are uniquely you, and don't ever forget it.

But kids can feel this kind of criticism so deeply. I remember at one of these events a girl of about twelve or thirteen who said to me, "I'm fat, I'm ugly, and I'm worthless." I wasn't going to let her get away with thinking anything like that.

"For one thing," I said, "you're big and beautiful. For another, you're not worthless—you're a diamond in the rough. You just gotta take a little grease and shine that diamond." We sat there and talked. She said, "I'm going to lose weight because everybody calls me fat." I said to her, "I want you to rephrase that. I want you to say, 'I'm going to lose weight because I love myself and I'm doing this for me and nobody else.'"

"Why would I say that?" she wanted to know.

"Because you don't ever want to do something just because somebody else told you to do it."

Then I asked her to sing with me, and I started singing "Amazing Grace." She joined in right away, and when we had finished, I said to her, "How can you tell me that out of what you consider an 'ugly' person came that beautiful voice? The beauty that I just heard in your voice comes from your soul, and it makes you as beautiful outside as you are inside." That's what I try to tell the kids I talk to—that their beauty starts within themselves.

THIS IS my life's work—to keep on talking about abuse and its impact and ways to prevent it or stop it or recover from it. Although I always try to tailor my message to the audience I'm speaking to, there are three core messages I try to bring home to all audiences: first, listen; second, speak up; and third, look for signals.

Listening first. This is the message I drive home again and again to teachers and school administrators, police officers, medical personnel—all the people who represent some kind of authority. By law all of them are required to report any sort of suspected child abuse to Child Protective Services, which is then obligated to investigate the matter. Different states have different laws about the procedures for doing all this, but there is no such thing anywhere as a "protocol" requiring that you can't send parents out of the room and talk to children on their own.

When I think back to the teachers and social workers and doctors who did basically nothing when I asked for help as a child, it seems to me that all of them disobeyed federal law. To me, that says that they didn't care or they decided I was making it up or they *did not want to get involved*. Whatever the reason, they weren't doing their jobs.

But these are the people children will talk to if they can. They *are* "authority." They wear the uniforms that say they have the power to help: a cop's blue shirt and badge, a doctor's white coat and stethoscope, a nurse's cap, a teacher's place at the desk up front with the power to keep you after school. These are the people children look up to, and when the people children look up to don't come to their aid, it tells them that no one will, that they're on their own, and that they just have to put up with what's happening to them.

We need to train our teachers and counselors, our social workers and police officers to make kids feel safe when they ask for help, and the first step in doing that is to take what they say seriously—*not* to tell them to go home and talk to Mom or Dad. In fact, when kids are ready to talk about their abuse, make the parents leave the room. That's the only way the child will speak openly, freely, and without fear. You can always decide later that the child was exaggerating or making it up or just looking for attention. That happens, of course. But it isn't nearly as damaging a sin as abuse is, and for the child being abused, you, the person in authority, are the first stop on the way to ending the abuse. I showed what I now know were clear signs of abuse. It would have been life changing if someone had believed me.

I know that the attitudes and actions of people in authority are changing, and I want to be part of that change. I frequently give talks to police officers and social workers who are committed to finding more and better ways to keep an eye and an ear out for kids in the kind of trouble I was in. I wish more medical personnel and teachers could attend some of the workshops I participate in that focus on these issues.

But I tell all grownups: listen to children. Not just to what they're saying but also to what they're *not* saying. Listen to the way they talk about home or family. Ask about how they feel. Pay attention to their body language. And listen *hard*. A kid who is being bullied in school is already so cut off from his classmates that he probably won't want to answer a question about whether he is being bullied. Please don't leave it there; don't take "Yes, I'm fine" for an answer. Because believe me when I say that the thoughts and feelings inside a child being bullied can be dangerous, both for the kid and for those bullying him.

It is always a good idea to follow up on a child's claim of abuse or bullying rather than to dismiss it. You can always dismiss it later. But a teacher who decides for himself that the bruises on a kid in his class are just the way the kid's family disciplines bad behavior may be missing something. The same goes for the emergency room physician who is "too busy" to ask questions when a kid is brought in black and blue all over. So when I speak to any group of people in authority, I'm not there to remind them of their responsibility—they know their responsibility. I'm there to tell them what it feels like to be a child when grownups who are in a position to help avoid their responsibility or just run away from it.

To kids themselves, I say: listen to your gut feeling, especially if you feel like there's something wrong and even if you are just not sure. For example, I tell them: you might start walking down a side alley because it's the quickest route to where you're going, but then your gut tells you to turn around. When that happens, do what your gut tells you to do. It's better to take more time and arrive late than to get stuck in a situation you don't want to be in.

Second, speak up. Kids often want to tell others what they're going through, and to them I say: keep telling it. If nobody hears you the first time, don't be afraid to tell it again and again and again until somebody hears you. Remember that getting hurt is not your fault! So don't wait. Hiding the pain only protects the person who hurt you and lets that person hurt others.

Grownups can be even more reluctant than kids to speak up. Women in damaging relationships are often afraid or ashamed to tell someone. They're worried their partner will find out and take it out on them by exercising even tighter control or carrying out more violent beatings. Or they're terrified he might take it out on their children. Or they are mortified to be caught out, having "chosen" this man as a partner.

Tell someone anyway—no matter what you think the cost might be, no matter how guilty or embarrassed or stupid you feel. Delay just raises the cost of silence. It gives your abuser more time to cause more damage and just makes the whole situation worse.

Again, if the first person you tell doesn't believe you, tell someone else. Keep speaking up until someone believes you and comes to your rescue.

The women and girls who so bravely spoke up in 2017 about the abuse they suffered as children or about the toxic harassment that broke their professional dreams have taught us so much about the power of raising your voice. A rumble that keeps going can become a roar. The middle-aged women who have spoken up about abuse they experienced as children—the athletes telling about coaches or team doctors, the many women telling about abuse by relatives— have all helped make it that much easier for children being abused now to speak up. I applaud them, and I hope they will join with me in continuing to tell our stories wherever and whenever there is anyone to listen—and for as long as it takes to create change. For when it comes to abuse of any kind, silence is the great enabler. Please don't stay silent. Say "me too." Speak up.

Finally, look for signals. Abuse doesn't just happen suddenly. The statistics say that most abusers were abused themselves. They didn't get help, and they were not able to cope, so they fell back on inflicting on others the same kind of cruelty they were experiencing. But whatever the cause, if you look back after abuse has happened, you can usually see where it started. There are always telling signs.

This is certainly true for signs of abuse in kids. Kids who show signs of withdrawal—who hang back against the fence during recess, staying away from the other kids and their activities—may well be suffering abuse. The same goes for kids who are just the opposite—too aggressive or too active. If a kid's grades suddenly tank, that's a sign. If a child seems fearful or depressed, that too is a sign.

Frequent absences from school are a sign, and so is the kid who seems to never want to go home. A kid who wears the same clothes for a week or looks unwashed may be coming from an abusive atmosphere where there is no supervision. "Inappropriate" clothing is another sign: kids in thick sweaters or wearing head wraps or other odd clothing to cover themselves, or kids unwilling to use the gym shower may be trying to cover up their wounds from being beaten or from cutting themselves. That's what I did to cover the cutting I did to myself—wore big sweaters, whatever the weather. When I finally gave up cutting, I used rubber bands to flip against my skin and wore a bunch of them around my wrist so I would have them handy. Flipping a rubber band was an action *I* controlled. It meant I could direct the pain onto my body myself instead of the abuser doing it to me. So a kid with rubber bands around her wrist could be a signal.

It may be tougher to read the signs with grownups, who have more resources or more practice putting up a front. For instance, say you're visiting with a woman friend, and she keeps getting phone calls and texts from her husband or partner: *Where are you? Who are you with? When are you coming home? What time?*

In a way, it can seem romantic—like he just can't bear to be apart from her and can hardly wait until they're together again. But if he keeps calling, maybe every hour—*Why aren't you here yet? Don't be late. Do* not *be late*—that isn't romance; it's abuse. It's how he exerts control over her.

Or say you're trying to set up a girls' night out, and one friend says she needs to know how much it will cost so she can gather the right amount of cash. No, she doesn't have a credit card—only her partner does—and she relies on a limited allowance from him. Also, she would need a ride because she has no access to the family car. In the end, she decides she'd better not come at all. Warning signs, all of them: no money and no car equals no mobility, and that means no freedom. She might as well have her feet tied together; she really can't move on her own—a sign of excessive control.

Abusers actually wave red flags as well. An early sign of an abuser—and this is something that pains me a lot—is abuse of small animals. Even little kids can easily gain control over frogs or bunnies or kitties. If they exercise that control in cruel ways, they're already in trouble. Unless somebody intervenes and gets through to them, they will simply escalate to bigger animals—and then to humans. I have seen the awful evidence of this in my own life. My family abused small animals first, then their own dogs, then their own children. Ariel Castro killed my puppy, but he'd been abusing animals long before. He abused his wife; he abused us. There was no one to stop him, so the abuse kept spiraling up and up.

If you see kids showing cruelty to animals—which is against the law, by the way—it is time to alert someone or set something in motion that may be able to turn those kids away from their path of cruelty and the destination it almost certainly leads to.

I know that sometimes it can seem that everything is a sign of abuse. And if you are an individual who doesn't have the authority or training of a cop or a social worker, it's hard to know how to act on what you hear or see or think. You're on a bus going somewhere, and you see a kid with bruises, and you wonder if he fell off his bike or if he's being hit by a parent. What's your responsibility as an individual and a stranger? That's hard to figure out.

Still, better safe than sorry. If you see something, say something. That goes especially for people in authority, because for them, the standards are pretty clear. And from where I'm looking at it, there's a special place in hell for people who hear about or suspect child abuse and then do nothing about it.

ONE DAY at a time. After the darkness I take my life one day at a time. I think those of you who have survived your own darkness know what I mean.

One day at a time, we remind ourselves never to belittle what we went through and never to deny the pain. Every day we remember how far down inside ourselves we had to reach to find enough hope to fight for survival that day. We can do that again if we need to.

One day at a time, I remind myself that my past does not define me and that I have the power to turn things around.

Each day I walk out the door to new and exciting experiences. But I remember what it was like to be afraid to walk outside, and to fear that I would never come back.

One day at a time, I take up the fight to forgive so that I can open my heart. And I fight to remember that forgiveness can take time.

Every day is a struggle, and every day is a learning experience. Every day those of us who have survived the darkness must promise not to give up on ourselves. If we make a mistake, we have to try to learn from it and give ourselves some grace. Every day we must remember that what we went through was not our fault.

We *can* be happy. I have found that the light I walked into after all that darkness offers so many possibilities for happiness. Just to be with my sweetie, to draw what I choose to draw, to write whatever I want to write whenever I want, to start each day with my cup of coffee, out in the backyard, just taking in what I see, hear, and can feel all around me . . .

Acknowledgments

I want to start by thanking everyone for all the love, support, donations, gifts, and prayers. It was because of you that I was able to start a new life. I want you to know I am healthy and happy. Yes, I went through hell and back, but I survived. I do not let the situation define me. I define the situation. And I hope that I can inspire other survivors to do the same.

I want to thank my literary agent, Lacy Lynch; my public relations representative, Lorraine Schuchart; and my lawyer, Christina Evans, for their dedication, guidance, and support in telling this story.

Thanks to the Dupree/Miller team: CEO Jan Miller, Shannon Marven, Nena Madonia, Donald Griffin, and the rest of the team for your advocacy and early championship of me and my cause.

I also want to thank the team at Hachette Book Group: Amanda Murray, Georgina Levitt, and Mollie Weisenfeld.

Appreciation goes to Susanna Margolis and Lorraine Schuchart for help in writing this book.

I want to acknowledge the entire team at Prosper for Purpose for their direction and support over the past two years.

I am grateful to Hahn Loeser & Parks for helping me create my team of advisers.

This book would not have been possible without my safe circle: my true friends. Thank you for believing in me, for being there when I needed you, for accepting me for who I am. I am truly blessed to have you in my life.

To the love of my life, you have played a major part of my life. You have stood by my side, despite any obstacles I have faced. You have always believed in me, especially when others didn't. You have accepted me without judgment and loved me unconditionally. I am truly blessed to have you to share my sunrise and sunset with.

Appendix: Resources

CRISIS HOTLINES

Childhelp National Child Abuse
1-800-4-A-Child
(1-800-422-4453)

National Runaway Safeline
1-800-789-2929

National Sexual Assault Telephone Hotline
1-800-656-HOPE (4673)

National Domestic Violence Hotline
1-800-799-SAFE (7233)
Report your situation without saying a word at
www.thehotline.org

National Human Trafficking Resource Center
1-888-373-7888 or
Text Help to 233733

PROGRAMS, ADVOCACY, RESEARCH

American Bar Association Commission on
Domestic & Sexual Violence
www.americanbar.org
Addressing domestic and sexual violence from the legal
perspective, the Commission seeks to increase access to justice
for survivors by engaging the interest and support of members of
the legal profession.

Battered Women's Justice Project
www.bwjp.org
Develops and promotes policy and practice innovations that
improve the response to intimate partner violence.

Futures Without Violence
futureswithoutviolence.org
Health and social justice nonprofit with the mission to heal those
among us who are traumatized by violence today—and to create
healthy families and communities free of violence tomorrow.

National Center on Domestic and Sexual Violence
www.ncdsv.org
Provides and customizes training and consultation, influences
policy, promotes collaboration, and enhances diversity with the
goal of ending domestic and sexual violence.

National Center for Missing and Exploited Children
www.missingkids.com
The nation's clearinghouse and comprehensive reporting center
for all issues related to the prevention of and recovery from

child victimization, NCMEC leads the fight against abduction, abuse, and exploitation—because every child deserves a safe childhood.

National Network to End Domestic Violence
www.nnedv.org
Advocacy organization comprising state domestic violence coalitions and allied organizations and individuals working to understand the needs of domestic violence victims and programs, and to voice those needs to national policymakers.

National Organization for Victim Assistance
www.trynova.org
The nation's leading advocacy organization for crime victims and those who serve them.

No More
www.nomore.org
Unites and strengthens a diverse, global community to help end domestic violence, sexual assault, and abuse.

Rape, Abuse & Incest National Network
www.rainn.org
The nation's largest anti-sexual violence organization, RAINN works to prevent sexual violence, help survivors, and help bring perpetrators to justice.

V-Day
www.vday.org
A global activist movement to end violence against women and girls. Founded by Tony-winning playwright Eve Ensler, V-Day

stages creative events to increase awareness, raise funds, and support anti-violence organizations.

OHIO-BASED

The Cleveland Rape Crisis Center
Cleveland Rape Crisis Center's mission is to support survivors of rape and sexual abuse, promote healing and prevention, and advocate for social change. Our vision is the elimination of sexual violence. Each year, the Center serves more than 36,000 with the operation of 14 satellite offices in Northeast Ohio. 24-Hour Hotline (216) 619-6192 or (440) 423-2020.

Domestic Violence & Child Advocacy Center (DVCAC)
The mission of the Domestic Violence & Child Advocacy Center is to empower individuals, educate the community, and advocate for justice to end domestic violence and child abuse. 24-Hour Hotline (216) 391-HELP (4357)

Project STAR (Sex Trafficking Advocacy & Recovery)
Provides expert, trauma-informed crisis intervention, advocacy, and counseling to survivors of sex trafficking in Ohio. Advocates meet survivors in a safe place (hospital, police station, shelter) to provide support after they are recovered from, or have left, a trafficking situation. To schedule an appointment, call the Intake Line at (216) 619-6194 ext. 141 or request an appointment online: https://clevelandrapecrisis.org/contact/request-an-appointment.

IDENTITY-SPECIFIC

Incite!
www.incite-national.org
Nationwide network of radical feminists of color working to
end violence against women, gender nonconforming, and trans
people of color and our communities.

Jewish Women International
jwi.org
The leading Jewish organization working to empower women
and girls by ensuring and protecting their physical safety and
economic security.

Manavi
www.manavi.org
The word means "primal woman" in Sanskrit, and this women's
rights organization is committed to ending violence against and
exploitation of South Asian women living in the United States
through direct service to survivors, community activism, and
awareness programs.

Mending the Sacred Hoop
www.mshoop.org
Working from a social change perspective to end violence
against Native women and children while restoring their safety,
sovereignty, and sacredness.